D0057436

Puritanism in
Old and New England

"Temporal things will have their weight in the World, and tho Zeal may prevail for a time, and get the better in a Skirmish, yet the War endeth generally on the side of Flesh and Blood, and will do so until Mankind is another thing than it is at present."

SIR GEORGE SAVILE, MARQUIS OF HALIFAX
The Character of a Trimmer

Puritanism in
Old and New England

ALAN SIMPSON

THE UNIVERSITY OF CHICAGO PRESS
CHICAGO AND LONDON

CHARLES R. WALGREEN FOUNDATION LECTURES

THE UNIVERSITY OF CHICAGO PRESS, CHICAGO 60637

The University of Chicago Press, Ltd., London

Copyright 1955 by The University of Chicago. All rights reserved
Published 1955. Eighth Impression 1972. Printed in the
United States of America

International Standard Book Number: 0–226–75929–6

Library of Congress Catalog Card Number: 55–13637

Foreword

OUR notion of Puritanism robust in its day has been
advanced sharply by modern scholars. The Puritan
of history is not to be typified only as a grim visage over
a cold conscience but as a human being with consequent
strength and weakness. Despite the severity of his doctrines, he inherited a Christian past of love and mercy.
The Puritan laid the foundation of enduring American
institutions, and today his influence still penetrates our
society.

Professor Simpson's study soundly appraises the
Puritan experience in politics on two continents.

JEROME G. KERWIN, *Chairman*
Charles R. Walgreen Foundation for the
Study of American Institutions

Preface

THIS book is composed of six lectures given under the Charles R. Walgreen Foundation at the University of Chicago in the spring of 1954. Only slight changes have been made in the form in which the lectures were originally delivered.

My object was to sketch the impact of Puritanism on English and American institutions in the seventeenth century and to end with a brief appraisal of the Puritan tradition. So far as any novelty lay in the point of view, it was to be found in the preoccupation with Puritanism as a species of enthusiasm with its own sources of inspiration and frustration. Such an attitude was a commonplace to Hume, Macaulay, and Guizot. It lost some of its sharpness in the narratives of Gardiner and Firth and was almost submerged by the modern cult for economic interpretations; but it revives in anyone who submits himself without prejudice to the record of Puritan aspiration in life and literature. Among scholars in recent times it has been best kept alive by those who have approached history through literature, and, while not forgetting my many obligations elsewhere, I would like to acknowledge a special debt to the works of Professor Perry Miller of Harvard University and of Professor A. S. P. Woodhouse of the University of Toronto.

A. S.

CHICAGO

[vi]

Table of Contents

✦ I ✦

The Puritan Thrust

How does one define Puritanism? No doubt there is a sense in which Puritanism can be found in the Middle Ages or in civilizations other than our own; but I am concerned here with the historic experiences from which the name derives. It began as a sneer, was taken up in self-defense, and has established itself as a convenient label. But historians have differed widely in its usage. There is one tradition which restricts it to the more orthodox branches represented by Presbyterianism in England and Congregationalism in New England.[1] Boston, with a vested interest in its own respectability, has often inclined to this usage. There is another tradition which extends it through the Center and Left of the movement but stops short at the Quakers.[2] For my own part, if I am looking at the movement as a whole, I can see little reason for excluding the Quakers. An enterprise which began in the sixteenth century by exhorting men to prepare themselves for a miracle of grace and ended by asserting the presence of the Holy Spirit in every individual is one movement. If it has many stopping places en route, it has a logical terminus. If one movement requires one label, and if one is not to go to the trouble of inventing a new one, I am content to apply the term "Puritan" to the whole of it. However,

it is not the name that matters but the unity, or continuity of experience,[3] that underlies the labels.

What was it that they all shared? The formal answer
is dissatisfaction within the established church—the
church established by Queen Elizabeth as the English
answer to the problems created by the Reformation,
the middle way between Rome and Geneva. This
answer is true enough but not the most revealing. A
better answer is one which seizes on the religious experience from which the dissatisfaction springs. The
essence of Puritanism—what Cromwell called the "root
of the matter"[4] when he surveyed the whole unruly
flock—is an experience of conversion which separates
the Puritan from the mass of mankind and endows
him with the privileges and the duties of the elect. The
root of the matter is always a new birth, which brings
with it a conviction of salvation and a dedication to
warfare against sin.

There is no difficulty in discovering what this experience involved. The whole object of the Puritan's
existence was to trace its course in himself and to produce it in others. He develops it in his sermons, systema-
tizes it in his creeds, charts it in his diaries. Of innumer-
able examples, let me describe the experience of Thomas
Goodwin; rather, let me summarize his own description.[5] He wrote it, of course, for edification; and, if it
was not published in his lifetime, we can easily imagine
how many sermons were based on it and how many
students of Magdalen College, over which he eventually
presided, were given the opportunity of benefiting
from it.

The Goodwin home, in which he was brought up,

had its face set in the right direction. The family stance seems to have been like that of Bunyan's Pilgrim, with the burden on his back, the Book in his hands, and the cry ringing in his ears, "What shall I do to be saved?" At six, young Thomas was warned by a servant that, if he did not repent of his sins, Hell awaited him. At seven, he had learned to weep for them and look for the signs of grace. At twelve, he thought he had more grace than anyone else in his village. At thirteen, he went up to Christ's College, Cambridge, and attached himself, as an eager learner, to the more mature laborers in the vineyard. He learned of the ministries of Perkins and Ames. He heard of famous conversions. He joined the spiritual exercises which the faculty held in their rooms. He was taught, with other students, how to test the state of his soul. This was the life which he was to try to institutionalize in Oxford under the Cromwellian government and which a profane generation was to describe as Goodwin's scruple-shop; but meanwhile he was a beginner and for many years a beginner oscillating between hope and despair. For the real experience had not yet come.

He kept on thinking he had it, only to find himself deceived. He could go through all the cycle of self-examination, repentance, exaltation, and good works, only to discover that the sense of assurance evaporated. The elect kept their assurance. The doctrine not only said so: one had only to look at them to see. But he lost his. For a time Arminianism offered its consolations. Arminianism was that doctrine of free will which was asserting itself everywhere as a reaction against predestination and was coming to be the distinguishing mark of the official piety at the time Goodwin was a student. For a time this Arminianism seemed to square with his experience. If the human will was not enslaved by sin but free to choose, he ought to expect the sense of assurance to fluctuate. But in his heart he knew that Arminianism was wrong because the holy youths do not fall away. They persevere, showing that God has indeed seized them. At this point he faltered in his pilgrimage and surrendered, as he tells us, to his characteristic sin. If salvation eluded him, success was well within his reach. The holy preachers like Dr. Sibbes, the holy converts like Mr. Price, the holy tutors, and the holy students could go on brooding over their consciences. Thomas Goodwin would stick to a fashionable style and make his mark.

He explains that he was saved from the consequences of this depraved decision by the real experience. It came to him, of course, through the medium of a sermon: the normal means employed by God to hammer the hardened heart. The text was "Defer not thy repentance." As he describes it, the characteristic features of the experience emerge. He is completely passive, for this is a Divine power exerted on a soul which is incapable of helping itself. He is shown *how* incapable by a revelation of his unworthiness which distinguishes the real thing from previous illusions. He compares the light shed by grace upon the state of a natural man's soul with the light of the sun piercing into the depths of a filthy dungeon to reveal a floor crawling with vermin. Always before, when he wept for his sins, he had kept some feeling of human merit. Now he knows he has none; that the natural man, even when seemingly a good man, is only a beautiful abomination, for the natural man has had no merit since Adam's disobedience, and Hell is his just destination. Then, in the midst of this horror, comes the act of mercy: the voice that says to the dead soul, "Arise and live." Goodwin compares himself to a traitor whom a king has pardoned and then raised to the position of friend and favorite. But, if the favorite has tremendous privileges, he also has tremendous duties. His life must be an endless war against the sin which dishonors his sovereign and an endless effort to be the means of producing in others that experience which has freed himself.

I could, of course, have chosen better-known personages than Thomas Goodwin, for there is almost no famous Puritan who has not left some account of this experience, even though it is only, as in Cromwell's case, a few haunted lines written to a cousin in the midst of his travail.[6] I chose Goodwin because he is typical,[7] because he is writing deliberately for imitation, and because he illustrates one of the characteristic weaknesses of the Puritan character—its want of proportion.

However Puritans differ, they all have something in common with Thomas Goodwin. They separate the world of nature from the world of grace. They insist that the natural man cannot grow in grace; he has to be reborn. They explain the rebirth as a vivid personal experience in which the individual soul encounters the wrath and redemptive love of God. It is an experience for which the church may prepare a man, and after which it may claim to guide him, but which in its essential nature is beyond the church's control. They describe the new creature in the language appropriate to a special destiny: he is the elect, the chosen, the favorite, the peculiar people,[8] the saint. They extol the liberty of the new creature, by which they mean the gift of eternal life, and the freedom which the regenerate may claim on earth under Divine law. It is the duty of the saint to search out that law and live by it, and, no matter how much they differ, they are agreed about one thing. It demands discipline. The discipline of self-trial—the perpetual self-accusation of the Puritan diaries; the discipline of self-denial—the massive prohibitions of the Puritan code; the discipline which Milton found in Cromwell when he said he could conquer the world because he had first conquered himself.[9] In later generations what they were talking about could be confused with respectability; but in these days it was a holy violence under compression. Finally, they derive this view of life from the Scriptures, which they regard as the sole source of authority—the complete rule by which men must live—though we shall see later how some regenerate spirits contrive to escape from this initial limitation.

This doctrine of salvation was a logical development, on English soil, of the Protestant doctrines of predestination, justification by faith, and the all-sufficiency of the Scriptures. Whether it stems, as older historians were content to say, from Calvinism or, as we now tend to say, from Rhineland Protestantism,[10] it is enough to recognize that, in the opinion of those who held it, the whole movement of history which we call the Reformation, and which they regarded as a Divine liberation of the church from centuries of superstition, was intended to have this result.

They lived, however, in a society which obviously thought otherwise. When the Puritan looked around him in Elizabethan England, he saw two kinds of wickedness: the wickedness of people who were living without any benefit from religion and the wickedness of people who had embraced the wrong religion. The first class had always been a considerable section of mankind in the most Christian centuries. In this century of religious confusion, social disturbance, intellectual speculation, and fierce acquisitive energy, godlessness confronted the Puritan in every walk of life. He met it on the Elizabethan roads, in those rogues and vagabonds who exemplified the modern problem of poverty. He met it in the underworld of the overgrown capital. He heard it in the announcement of businessmen that clergymen ought not to meddle with a merchant's business. Ordinary humanity in its alehouse; the crowd that thronged the Shakespearean theater; the intellects released from Christian tradition; the court with its worship of beauty, wit, honor, power, and fame—all seemed dedicated to the proposition that men are created without a soul to be saved or damned. Some insight into this world—or at least into its less sophisticated reaches—is provided by a list of thirty-two popular errors which William Perkins, a founder of the Puritan discipline, catalogued for the instruction of the ignorant.[11] It is a comprehensive indictment of the profane, the cheerful, the superstitious, the free-enterprisers, and the people who thought it enough to be good citizens. Here are some of the items in this syllabus of errors:

"Drinking in the alehouse is good fellowship and shews a good kind nature, and maintains neighbourhood."

"Howsoever a man live, yet if he call upon God on his death bed, and say Lord have mercy upon me, and so go away like a lamb, he is certainly saved."

"Merry ballads and books, such as *Scogin*, *Bevis of Southampton*, etc., are good to drive away time and remove heart qualms."

"A man may go to wizards, called wisemen, for counsel; because God hath provided a salve for every sore."

"Every man must be for himself and God for us all."

"A man may make of his own [property] whatsoever he can."

"If a man be no adulterer, no thief, nor murderer, and do no man harm, he is a right honest man."

This last seems an innocent sentiment until we recall that from Perkins' point of view this man is simply a beautiful abomination so long as he remains an unconverted soul.

This unregenerate world would not be allowed to flaunt its wickedness if religion were rightly understood. But what was the official religion? The Puritan found himself confronted by that Anglican piety which had developed side by side, and in conflict with his own, within the framework of the Establishment erected by Queen Elizabeth. The famous settlement of the first year of her reign had left a great deal unsettled, but the complexion which it finally acquired was thoroughly frustrating to the Puritan. He believed in the total depravity of nature; he was told that men were not so fallen as he thought they were. He believed that the natural man had to be virtually reborn; he was told that he could grow in grace. He believed that the sermon was the only means of bringing saving knowledge and that the preacher should speak as a dying man to dying men. He was told that there were many means of salvation, that sermons by dying men to dying men were often prolix, irrational, and socially disturbing, and that what they had to say that was worth saying had usually been better said in some set form that could be read aloud. He demanded freedom for the saints to exercise their gifts of prayer and prophecy, only to be told that the needs of the community were better met by the forms of common prayer. He felt instinctively that the church was where Christ dwelt in the hearts of the regenerate. He was warned that such feelings threatened the prudent distinction between the invisible church of the saved and the visible church of the realm. He insisted that the church of the realm should be judged by Scripture, confident that Scripture upheld him, and prepared to assert that nothing which was not expressly commanded in Scripture ought to be tolerated in the church. He was told that God had left much to the discretion of human reason; that this reason was exercised by public authority, which in England was the same for both church and state; and that whatever authority enjoined, in its large area of discretion, ought to be loyally obeyed.

Obviously what we have here is a reconstruction of a

Catholic tradition within the framework of a national Protestant church. As stated here, it is derived from Richard Hooker, who was writing at a time when most Anglican bishops still subscribed to that theology of predestination whose implications the Puritans were rigorously pursuing. But the Establishment had clearly refused to take this path, and before long they adopted the Arminianism which was much more congenial to them.

The effect of these tendencies on the Puritan can easily be imagined. Such a church had misconceived the "root of the matter." At best, it was a halfway house between a corrupt and a pure church; at worst, it was barely distinguishable from Rome. It was not run by saints; it was not organized for the production of saints; and it did not repress the world's wickedness.

What were the elect to do? The first thing they could do was to organize, using every available means for the infiltration of English life and the conversion of authority to their point of view. They had plenty of opportunities, both in the early days, when the character of the settlement was relatively undetermined, and later. The powers which could be brought to bear on dissidents in this society were limited even when fully deployed. Aristocracy imposed its shelter between the individual and the state; so did corporate bodies like the universities, the Inns of Court, the commercial companies, and the municipalities. Above all, Parliament was open to the efforts of the Reformers, and, though the sovereign's disfavor for any interference with his ecclesiastical supremacy was obvious enough, there were hopes that he might see the light. Could he resist the plain word of God? So for three generations Puritans organized, with a base in the universities, a grip on the press, a connection in the country houses and the counting-houses, and a party in Parliament. It was an advancing frontier of preachers, converts, and patrons, checked by many features in the social topography but always pushing forward to its goal—the completion of a half-finished Reformation.

Naturally, one asks what made people receptive to such a demanding view of life, and naturally there have been suggestions that this doctrine of salvation was somehow connected with the aspirations of social classes. We have been told, with varying degrees of crudity and subtlety, that Puritanism was the ideology of the bourgeoisie.[12] On that subject there are two simple observations to be made. First, Puritanism never offered itself as anything but a doctrine of salvation, and it addressed itself neither directly nor indirectly to social classes but to man as man. Second, its attractions as a commitment were such that it made converts in all classes—among aristocrats, country gentry, businessmen, intellectuals, freeholders, and small tradesmen. Earls were linked with tinkers in the fraternity of converted souls. However, some of the preachers' seed fell on stony ground, and some fell on ground in which it would never have germinated without artificial stimulants. High society and slum society were, on the whole, stony ground. So also were the field laborers, for the reasons that Baxter, who knew his parish as well as any clergyman in England, pointed out.[13] Puritanism was the religion of a Book, and, without opportunity to master the Book and to engage in mutual criticism

and edification around it, it was hard to make any progress. Weavers at their looms, tradesmen in their shops,
and yeomen farmers in their homes could be organized,
but not so easily the peasant in the field.

The fertilized ground was the ground which for one
reason or another was out of sympathy with official
policy: noblemen out of favor at court and ready to play
with Puritanism as a weapon or a consolation; country
gentry having a hard time making ends meet during a
century of inflation; city men irritated by royal or
episcopal regimentation or casting their eyes on church
lands; self-made men in rural industry who smarted
under the snubs of neighboring gentry; rural crafts-
men for whom there was either no church at all or
some country tippler mumbling a prayer between visits
to the alehouse; and Englishmen in all classes when the
strongest national prejudice—fear of popery—swept
across them and it looked as though safety lay in
embracing the other extreme. Genuine Puritans, as I
have defined them, were never more than a small
minority, but there was plenty of discontent on which
they could feed, and the movement grew with the years
as the country headed toward a crisis in the relations
between king and Parliament. The growth of a constitutional opposition to the Stuart monarchy had a separate origin from the Puritan movement, but it naturally
furnished the Puritan with his best hope of procuring a
reform of the church.

However, the more persistently the Puritan organized, the clearer it became that his attempt to remodel
the church would be resisted to the limit of the government's capacity. Elizabeth had administered the first

checks when the tendencies of the movement became plain. Once Puritans began to argue that church and state must be separated in England to the extent of putting the church on its scriptural basis, they ran into unflinching resistance. This was to separate the inseparable; to make the head of the state a member of some sort of Presbyterian church; and to place the state, in the final analysis, at the mercy of the interpreters of the Divine Will. However much they might protest that the monarchy had nothing to fear and everything to gain from a partnership with a scriptural church, Elizabeth knew better and suppressed them. Her successor, James I, who had had his own experience of Presbyterianism, followed suit with that mixture of hard words and half-hearted action that served him as a policy. Charles I put Archbishop Laud in charge. By 1630, when a wit was asked by a puzzled inquirer what the Arminians held—Arminianism being the badge of the Laudian party—he was able to reply, "All the best bishoprics and deaneries in England."[14] By that time, too, the partnership of king and bishop was "going it alone." Parliamentary government had been suspended after three unworkable Parliaments, and all the means of coercion were being marshaled against the Puritan allies of the constitutional opposition.

The reaction of the Puritans to this prolonged experience of frustration varied with the individual. It was their duty to search for the Will of God, which meant scanning his commands in Scripture, or applying to Scripture such reason as grace had restored, or following the lead of the spirit which dwelt in their hearts. What was the duty of a regenerate soul under an unregenerate government which persisted in maintaining a corrupt church? One reaction came early. It was nothing less than the fragmentation of the movement—the earliest symptoms of that process of fission which was to run through the whole history of Puritanism. The first impulse of the movement had been to think in terms of a national church, directed by the elite but embracing all members of the community: some English counterpart to the reformed churches of Scotland or the Continent. This continued to be the hope of the majority and eventually expressed itself in English Presbyterianism: the Puritanism of the Right. But in others frustration precipitated a potentiality inherent in the idea of election: the tendency to segregate the elite from the mass and to substitute for the traditional idea of a church coextensive with society the idea of a church as a covenanted body of saints. This was that pressure to identify the visible and the invisible church which figures so prominently in the Center and Left of the Puritan movement.

The impulse might be carried some way or all the way. Carried to its fullest extent, it meant separation: the duty to separate from the polluted mass of mankind. So little groups of saints peel off from the national church under the leadership of a minister to meet surreptitiously in each other's houses, to migrate to the Netherlands if England is made too uncomfortable for them, and to experience, wherever they go, the perplexities as well as the privileges of their strange adventure. Along this route, hovering between separation and some sense of communion with the church they had left, went the Pilgrim Fathers. Others were less

fortunate in their leadership. After beginning by reducing the church to a voluntary association, they
ended by reducing it to a collection of individuals, each
of whom had separated from the other's corruptions.
And so the Reformation achieved one of its logical
possibilities, with the individual becoming a church in
himself.

The same impulse carried only part way rejected
separation and continued to think in terms of an
orthodoxy imposed on the community; but the ecclesiastical medium would be an association of covenanted
churches, each composed of individuals who could give
satisfactory evidence of their conversion. A succession
of distinguished figures in this tradition also migrated
to the Netherlands, to work out there, so far as English and Dutch authority permitted, some of the implications of what we have come to call Nonseparating
Congregationalism.[15]

In this way, lines of fragmentation were being etched
out in the years of opposition. On the Right, the future
Presbyterians; in the Center, the future Congregationalists; on the Left, the Separating Congregationalists. In England, where all plans for the future of church
government had to be subordinated to the struggle for
survival of a preaching ministry, the distinctions might
be blurred. Abroad, where the tasks of organization had
to be faced, they emerged more sharply.

So the first response to frustration is the fragmentation of the movement, and another is the decision to
migrate. But what of those who remained? Ought they
to rebel? Puritans had never thought so. When an Elizabethan Puritan had his right hand cut off by the execu-

tioner for writing a pamphlet which the government had found seditious, he raised his hat with his left hand to cry, "God save the Queen!"[16] When Charles I suspended parliamentary government in 1629, it was still far from clear that God ever intended his saints to take up arms against constituted authority. Even in 1642, when king and Parliament faced each other in civil war, there were still some Puritans who would have held aloof if they had not been harried into parliamentary garrisons by a royalist rabble.[17] But by that time the bulk of them had been converted to the duty of resistance, and the neutrals could hardly be surprised if they found themselves hustled on the streets because their dress and deportment marked them out as fellow-travelers of the Puritans in arms.

This transformation of the loyal subject into a subversive, if not inevitable, was not surprising. Hobbes reflected the feelings of most contemporaries in the 1630's when he observed that men who placed their duty to God before their duty to the state were poor security risks.[18] Macaulay summed up the feelings of posterity when he seized on that quality in the Puritan's experience—his election—which made all terrestrial distinctions pale before the distinction between those who had looked on God's face and those who were lost in darkness.[19] Like the Reformers everywhere, the Puritan had taught himself the duty of passive obedience to the state so long as the state seemed likely to reform the church. Like them, he became a rebel after the state had frustrated him and a better prospect offered itself. In this English situation he could reach his decision by one of two routes. The first was to adopt the argument pleaded by his parliamentary allies: that under the English constitution, in a crisis between king and Parliament, a right resided in the Parliament to resist a conspiracy which had seized control of the royal government.[20] This was an argument which took him into the nature of political authority in general and of the English constitution in particular, for which nothing in his Puritan experience had especially prepared him, except the conviction that the truth must lie on the Parliament's side because that was where the interests of religion lay. The second route was more direct, and it was to have an ominous future. It consisted in persuading himself that the ordinary duties of obedience had been set aside by an extraordinary call to the saints. This was a doctrine which could be invoked to justify any violence until the embattled saints were dazed by the ruin they had caused.

So far I have been attempting to sketch the nature of the Puritan thrust as it developed in opposition. What use would the Puritan make of power? Just as it is possible to say that all Puritans shared a conversion experience, so it is possible to say that the Puritan thrust carried all Puritans into a determined effort to erect a holy community.[21] They discover a sense of mission to complete that tremendous process which God had begun with the Reformation—the liberation of his church from centuries of superstition and error. They throw themselves into this crusade with all the intense ardor of which the elect are capable. But what can be predicted about the shape of their holy community when the opportunity comes to embody the vision in institutions? Only this—that the grand object will be the regeneration of fallen man. Human history is the field in which God gathers his elect, and the success of the holy community will be measured by the production of saints—by that miracle of rebirth within the human soul which forms the great end of all Puritan striving and from which all other good things will flow. Beyond this affirmation of faith and purpose, all else is uncertain. As they face the problems involved in creating a political order fit for saints to live in, they will endeavor to discover the Will of God. But what will they find? Does God want a partnership of church and state for the enforcement of a Puritan orthodoxy? That is one possible answer—typified by Massachusetts and Right-wing Puritanism in England. Does he want a separation of church and state to protect the purity of the church and the peace of the state? That is another answer—typified by Rhode Island and the English separatists. Does he want a democratic republic, in which the government of the state will be modeled on the government of the democratic congregation? That is another answer—typified by the party to be known as Levellers in English history. Does he want a dictatorship of saints to inaugurate the millennium? That will seem a very exhilarating possibility amid the wreckage of the English Civil Wars. However, all this lies in the future, while the job in hand is to escape from, or to destroy, the regime which frustrates them all.

❧ II ❧
The Covenanted Community

T HE first chance to see what the Puritan saint would make of life, if he had the freedom to experiment, came in America. The early history of Massachusetts (together with that of Plymouth, Connecticut, and New Haven, for the differences are unimportant from our point of view) is the story of men who shared an ideal, left the Old World to realize it in the New, only to discover when the work of planting was done that the spirit had evaporated. Frustration was the fate which awaited every Puritan. In England, where the defeat came in war, it has all the features of tragedy; here, where there was no defeat but apparent success, it becomes a kind of ironic tale.

The Puritans who came to America continued to have much in common with those who stayed at home. Take, for instance, that apocalyptic view of their place in history which all Puritans shared and which can hardly be overemphasized if we want to understand the quality of their enthusiasm. We are all familiar today with the Communist's conviction that he is moving toward a preordained victory. His science tells him that the historical process is obeying a determinate logic, and, so far from the inevitability of this process slowing down his efforts, it acts as an enormous spur to them. The Puritan has a similar theory of history and the same sort of compulsion to cooperate with destiny. Admittedly, Divine Providence is a good deal more mysterious than dialectical materialism. But this unpredictability, if an argument in some situations for more patience than a Communist could admit in his timetable, always offers the possibility of a miraculous delivery. The winters of the church may be cruelly long; but when that frozen world thaws, as in the springtime of the Reformation, the whole earth seems to rush toward its harvest.

The Puritan thought of human history as the field in which God gathered his saints, saving the few from the fate which all had deserved and imparting to that few some knowledge of his Will. For reasons known only to himself, God had permitted ignorance of his Will to envelop the visible church between the age of the apostles and the age of the Reformation. These thirteen or fourteen centuries had seen a downward swing to the lowest depths of depravity; then a slow ascent had begun as God chose to reveal more and more of himself. Wave after wave of witnesses had been summoned to testify; country after country seemed likely to be the scene in which the destiny of the age would be fulfilled. On the crest of that movement stood the Puritan, with his "panting, longing, eager" desire to find the revelation completed in himself.[1] These adjectives are not mine, nor are they those of some simple enthusiast. They might be Oliver Cromwell's or John Milton's. They are, in fact, the words of John Cotton, the leading intellectual among the founders of the New England Way.

The Covenanted Community

Incidentally, the intellectual quality in the Puritan's piety can easily be overstated. When every compliment has been paid to Professor Miller's studies of Puritanism[2]—and I yield to no one in my admiration for those ingenious works—at least one gentle criticism may be made. He has told us too much about the Puritan mind and not enough about the Puritan's feelings. If the seventeenth-century Puritan, with his formal training in scholasticism, usually tries to give a rational account of his faith, it is the stretched passion which makes him what he is. They are people who suffered and yearned and strived with an unbelievable intensity; and no superstructure of logic ought to be allowed to mask that turmoil of feeling.

It may be said, of course, that the Puritan was better prepared for disappointment than most men and therefore less disposed to commit himself to a utopian dream. It was some such thought as this that led Professor Miller to say that a disillusioned Puritan is impossible to conceive.[3] Was it not the Puritan who had preached the arbitrariness of God and the depravity of man? Who was he to falter if the age missed what in his foolish pride he had allowed himself to believe was its destiny? I can only say this was not the mood of 1630, when the Pilgrims left England to build their Zion in the wilderness. It was not the mood of Oliver Cromwell when he told a Parliament of Puritan saints that they stood on the edge of the promises and the prophecies.[4] It was the Puritan's compromise with defeat, and when he finally made it—either in the despairing cry of the English Puritan, "God has spit in our faces,"[5] or in the melancholy dirge of the American Puritan at the end of the century—the crusade was finished.

The founders of New England not only shared the apocalyptic view of history with the Puritans whom they left behind. Their confession of faith, their search for regeneration and sanctification, their techniques of self-trial and self-denial, all spring from the same community of experience. A series of New England sermons explaining how God calls, justifies, and sanctifies his elect; a New England diary recording an agonizing search for the evidence of this work in the diarist's soul; New England's advice to educators on the education of a saint or to businessmen on the duty of combining "diligence in business with deadness to the world";[6] New England's conviction that every man is his brother's keeper; New England's persuasion that a good joke ought to be balanced with some savory morsel to keep merriment in its proper bounds; New England's cultivation of the Puritan art forms: the biography of the saint, the record of divine judgments, the history which weaves both into a narrative of God's blessings and punishments—all this, and much else, can be matched on both sides of the water. Behind it shines that vision which a tinker living on the ecstatic fringe of the movement described for all Puritans in the *Pilgrim's Progress*.

The specialty of the New England Way only emerged as its founders came to grips with the problems of embodying the vision in institutions. It is suggested by that analogy which was not confined to them but which acquired a more concrete and durable form in their experience than elsewhere: the analogy between themselves and the first people who were admitted into a covenant of grace with God. New England was to be a New Israel—a covenanted community. Its founders, who had already experienced in their own lives the sensation of being offered, and of accepting, the covenant of grace, were to form themselves into a community of saints for the enjoyment of God's ordinances and the elevation of their colony into the status of a chosen people. Such seemed to be the opportunity which God, working through the secondary causes which made colonization possible at this juncture of history, was offering to the regenerate. The labor of explorers, the greed of merchants, the ambition of kings, the pressure of persecution, the incidence of economic hardship, every motive and every capacity for colonization was but a web of contrivance designed by invisible hands for ends which only the elect could fathom. The interpretation of those ends in terms of a covenanted community begins with the famous sermon by Governor Winthrop in mid-ocean and only ends among the disenchantments of the late seventeenth century after desperate efforts to recall the wandering pilgrims to a proper sense of their destiny.

Let me quote Governor Winthrop's own words. They are taken from the sermon called "A Modell of Christian Charity," which was delivered on board the *Arabella:*

Thus stands the cause between God and us; we are entered into Covenant with him for this work; we have taken out a Commission; the Lord hath given us leave to draw our own Articles; we have professed to enterprise these actions upon these and these ends; we have hereupon besought him of favor and blessing. Now if the Lord shall please to hear us, and bring us in peace to the place we desire,

then hath he ratified this Covenant and sealed our Commission, and
will expect a strict performance of the Articles contained in it, but
if we shall neglect the observation of these Articles which are the
ends we have propounded, and dissembling with our God, shall
fall to embrace this present world and prosecute our carnal inten-
tions, seeking great things for our selves and our posterity, the Lord
will surely break out in wrath against us, be revenged of such a per-
jured people, and make us know the price of the breach of such a
Covenant.[7]

What this decision came to mean was the tribalization of the Puritan spirit. The goals of regeneration
and sanctification, common to Puritans everywhere,
were to be sought within a tribal community. Let me
sketch some of the implications of this conception as
it appeared to its authors.

First, no diversity of opinion in fundamentals would
be permitted within the tribe. Regenerate men, using
that faculty of reason which grace had restored, and
applying it to the Word of God as revealed in Scripture, could come to only one conclusion. Rightly informed consciences do not judge differently; they
concur. What they perceive is that regenerate men must
form their lives within an external discipline and co-
operate in enforcing that discipline on the unregenerate.
The mission of the elect is to uphold an orthodoxy.

The external discipline of the tribe would involve, in
Winthrop's words, "a due form of ecclesiastical and
civil government."[8] So far as the first was concerned,
all Puritans believed that the true form of ecclesiastical
government had been prescribed in Scripture, and what
these Puritans found in Scripture was authority for
confining church membership to "visible saints."
Churches would be composed of groups of converted
souls who formed a covenant among themselves to

create a church and who looked forward to a perpetual succession of saints who would enter the church
covenant as the work of conversion continued. The
orthodox idea of a church, whether in Anglican England
or Presbyterian Scotland, was a body coextensive with
the community, admission to which depended on baptism, subsequently confirmed by a profession of faith.
But this New England church is going to be built out
of the conversion experience, and it is assumed that a
subjective experience can be detected by objective
tests. However, there is one other class of members
attached to the church besides the converted. God's
covenant with Abraham had included not only Abraham but his seed. The children of the converted will be
admitted to baptism, in the expectation that they will
eventually be able to attest the conversion experience
and qualify for full membership.

These churches, around which the New England
towns will be built, are autonomous congregations.
The powers of church government were not given by
God to bishops, or to Presbyterian assemblies, but to
them. However, no anarchic consequences need be
feared from their autonomy. Rightly informed consciences reach the same conclusions; that is the essence
of the promise. Congregations are expected to consult
if they encounter difficulties, and erroneous consciences,
persisting in their errors, will find themselves opposed
by the massed forces of orthodoxy.

So much for the ecclesiastical discipline. But in a
covenanted community the discipline of the state must
also be directed by saints. It is true that all Puritans
talk about the separation of church and state, and this

is one of the things that distinguish them from all Anglicans. But nine out of ten Puritans only want to separate church and state in order to bind them together again. In other words, they have to break the indissoluble unity of church and state in Anglican England so as to get the church on its scriptural basis, Presbyterian or Congregational, as the case may be; but, once on that basis, they expect the state to uphold it, to be "the nursing father" of the church. Separation of church and state, in such a context, meant simply a division of functions between two partners with a tendency to reduce the state to a junior partner where the clergy claimed a superior insight into the Divine Will. In New England it was expected to be a partnership in unison, for church and state alike were to be dominated by saints.

The same compact among saints would underlie the civil government as it underlay the ecclesiastical government. The idea that political authority, while authorized by God, derives from the consent of the people was a familiar one in the English tradition, and Puritans invoked it to suit their purposes. The founders of Massachusetts were prepared to interpret their charter as a social covenant, and the communities which hived off from Massachusetts used the covenant device to launch their plantations. But the consent which is expressed in these compacts is not to be confused with any notion of popular sovereignty. Popular sovereignty is the grossest atheism in a Puritan universe governed by God. It is a consent to be governed according to the ordinances of God: an acceptance by saints of the political obligations of a chosen people.

The Covenanted Community

These compacts do not commit them to any particular form of government. Forms of civil government, unlike forms of ecclesiastical government, are not prescribed in Scripture, and there is no reason why English representative institutions and English common-law principles should not be admitted into the holy community provided they do not prevent saints from governing that community, from protecting its church, and from making such changes as are necessary to bring English legal custom in line with the laws of God. However, this is some proviso. It means that in a remote corner of His Majesty's realm there will be a group of one-party states, where access to power depends on evidence of conversion. Party politicians will uphold the party preacher; laws will be modified to suit the party ethic; the administration of law will not be embarrassed by procedural safeguards; and all deviationists will either repent or suffer expulsion.

So much for "the due form of ecclesiastical and civil government." One further decision will be necessary to underpin the stability of the whole enterprise: a crucial decision about the qualifications of the prophet in the chosen community. The Puritan way of life had been worked out by a learned clergy, and learning—the learning of the schools—had been regarded as an indispensable means for the discovery and the application of the Divine Will in the lives of the regenerate. However, Puritanism had preached that without grace reason was helpless, that the pilgrim must await the miracle which no merit on his part could produce, and that, once this miracle had been bestowed, Christ was "ingrafted" in his heart. Could these regenerate spirits be held within any bounds? Could reason, which had begun by abdicating its authority, reassert itself so as to insure that one true discipline which was God's design for men—or even to insure any society at all? The whole history of Puritanism is a commentary on its failure to satisfy the cravings which its preaching had aroused. It was forever producing rebellions against its own teachers: rebellions within the learned camp and rebellions from outside that camp against the assertion that learned reason had anything to teach the illuminated spirit.

How much of this the founders of the covenanted community foresaw is open to question. The history of the Reformation had been full of it, and they were always being reminded by their enemies of the risks they ran; but in the nature of things these risks would not be fully revealed until the opportunity came for the saint to claim his privileges—the opportunity so delightfully expressed by that admirer of Anne Hutchinson who said to Edward Johnson: "I'll bring you to a woman that preaches better gospel than any of your black-coats that have been at the Ninneversity."[9] However, whether they foresaw it or not, it is certain that they carried with them the ideal of a learned clergy, and everyone knows of their determination to reproduce on the frontier the basic intellectual institutions of the Old World: the school, the college, the library, and the press. What is less clear, perhaps, since Professor Morison wrote his history of Harvard, is the purpose of these institutions. The merits of that great work speak for themselves, but it has one small flaw. The author has tried, in devious ways, to redeem his alma mater

from the suspicion of being too much troubled by sin.[10]
But the founders of Harvard College would hardly have
thanked him for this carnal enterprise. What they
aimed at producing was not Christian gentlemen with
a liberal education but saints with a saving knowledge.
The college was to be a school of prophets—learned
prophets, certainly, but emphatically prophets. What
else would a chosen people expect from its educational
institutions?

I have tried to sketch the lines along which the vision
would be embodied in these communities. Between 1630
and the mid-forties the work of planting and consolidat-
ing went on, until at last one species of Puritanism had
been stabilized. Viewed simply as an achievement of
order in the wilderness, out of human beings as po-
tentially explosive as Puritans, this was certainly impressive. But it is no slight to the leadership to suggest
that the problem of welding communities out of Puritan material was somewhat simplified for them.

The most obvious simplification was the opportunity
to create a new community without having to tear an
old one to pieces and to go on creating new communities if the first proved disappointing. These Puritans
leave all their opponents behind them. They pass
straight from settled life to the tasks of creating a
new life without any disorderly interlude. When they
reach the wilderness, work crowds in and danger binds
them. If the worse comes to the worst, there is always
the frontier. The deviationists can take their chances in
Rhode Island. Thomas Hooker, who is no deviationist,
but who may have felt that Massachusetts was too
small for two such redoubtable saints as himself and

Mr. Cotton, can become the founder of Connecticut. The saints in England must often have sighed for some such *Lebensraum*.

The other great advantage might seem to be the pre-agreement about ecclesiastical policy. Puritans had little difficulty in agreeing about doctrine. What they usually disagreed about was the form of church government within which the elect should fulfil their mission. When the Puritans came into power in England, they were prepared to fight a civil war over the rival merits of Presbyterianism, Nonseparating Congregationalism, and Separatism. New England, although it shares part of this experience in its contests with separatists like Roger Williams, rallies with surprising ease around the principle of Nonseparating Congregationalism and has relatively little difficulty with Presbyterianism. How did this happen?

It used to be thought that the adoption of Congregationalism was suggested by the example of Plymouth which the main body of the colonists found when they got there. It is now assumed that Professor Miller has conclusively demonstrated a pre-engagement among the majority of the clergymen which can be traced back through their Dutch experience to the original advocates of Nonseparating Congregationalism as a middle way between Presbyterianism and Separatism. However, Professor Miller has to admit that some ministers were Presbyterians; that others, who had not gone through the Dutch experience, might have been uncommitted, and that the views of the secular leaders, at the time of their arrival, are largely unknown.[11]

Doubtless the Congregationalists were in a position to

take the initiative. But the acquiescence in that initiative must certainly have been helped by the composition of the Puritan population that came over here and by the frontier situation. Congregationalism aroused objections in England as an unsuitable organization for a community which was both hierarchical and centralized. It deprived the great Puritan magnate of his power to appoint ministers. It seemed to place hereditary influence at the mercy of the conversion experience, for, unless his children could attest it, they would presumably find themselves deprived of both church membership and political power.[19] Worst of all, it looked like a dangerous loosening of the social bonds to substitute a church of autonomous congregations for the corporate and centrally controlled church of tradition. Just how dangerous was to become clear enough in the Civil Wars when Congregationalism, in its separatist form, became the medium through which every kind of radicalism found expression. But few of these fears were realistic in New England. Puritan peers and very rich Puritans, the backbone of English Presbyterianism, were conspicuous by their absence. The lesser leaders who came over were reasonably insured against social, as distinct from theological, unrest by their monopoly of talent and by the frontier opportunities which took the sting out of class bitterness. And the communities to be administered were, after all, a handful of decentralized settlements as compared with a highly integrated England. Congregationalism commended itself to clerical specialists like Cotton and Hooker as the one form of church government prescribed by God for his saints; but, if the local situation had not made it a safe enough proposition, the Word would doubtless have seemed less clear.

So much for the New England Way viewed simply as an achievement of order. But how far did it fulfil the expectations of its founders: that this covenanted people would represent the ideal toward which all history was converging; that there would be a succession of saints with the same intense piety as themselves; and that under the rule of these saints the whole community would be held to the obligations of the covenant and sanctified by its blessings?

Much of the frustration which follows is common to Puritans everywhere. They had dreamed of themselves as a united army forming the vanguard of history; but the army splinters into columns, battalions, and platoons, while history seems to be marching on. They had thought that conversion could become an institution, but they find themselves with church members where they had hoped for saints. They had devised one of the most formidable disciplines ever seen for keeping sin within bounds, but there seemed to be as much of it inside the covenant as outside. They had demanded an impossible tension from the elect and an impossible submission from the mass. Everywhere the taut springs relax, the mass rebels, and compromises eat away at a distinction on which the whole system was based.

The history of the New England Way is the history of a losing struggle to preserve the intensity of the experience of the saint and his authority over society. On the one hand, a church of visible saints, each of whom could attest the miracle of conversion, is gradually transformed into a church where membership depends on a profession of faith and a standard of Puritan morality. On the other hand, the church, thus formalized, is deprived of its organic control of political power and forced to depend for its control over society on the opportunity its clergy have had to make themselves a ruling class and the allies of ruling families.

The decay of spiritual intensity is the theme of almost all the founders as they survey the tribal community in their declining years. Few things are more moving than the comparisons drawn by a Bradford, a Winthrop, or a Shephard between the spirit that sustained them and the spirit they find around them.

Let me quote from Bradford—that simple hero who never forgot, in all the labor of planting a colony, that his true home was elsewhere. He had copied into his journal the claim which the leaders of their little church had made when they applied in 1617 for permission to settle in the New World:

> We are knit together as a body in a most strict and sacred bond and covenant of the Lord, of the violation whereof we make great conscience, and by virtue whereof we do hold ourselves straightly tied to all care of each other's good, and of the whole by every one, and so mutually.[13]

When he read that entry in his old age, he wrote this confession on the back of the page:

> O sacred bond, whilst inviolably preserved! How sweet and precious were the fruits that flowed from the same, but when this fidelity decayed, then their ruin approached. O that these ancient members had not died or been dissipated (if it had been the will of God) or else that this holy care and constant faithfulness had still lived, and remained with those that survived, and were in times afterward added unto them. But (alas) that subtle serpent hath slyly wound in himself under fair pretenses of necessity and the like

to untwist these sacred bonds and ties, and as it were insensibly, by degrees, to dissolve or in a great measure to weaken, the same. I have been happy, in my first times, to see, and with much comfort to enjoy, the blessed fruits of this sweet communion, but it is now a part of my misery in old age, to find and feel the decay and want thereof (in a great measure), and with grief and sorrow of heart to lament and bewail the same. And for others warning and admonition, and my own humiliation, do I here note the same.[14]

What had happened to them is part of the common experience of all creative revivals, when the first generation hands over to the second, when the organizer follows the visionary, and habit replaces direct experience as the source of guidance. But, of course, it is colored by their own circumstances. There is little to keep alive their memories of persecution. There is less and less to sustain their sense of the New World as a beacon for the Old when the progress of events in England reduces the New England Way first to a backwater of the Puritan spirit and later to a provincial anachronism. There is plenty of evidence that, in spite of all their precautions, worldliness is still with them and that saints who struggle to rule the world may find themselves ruled by it—especially the Puritan, who develops for religious purposes a type of character which can hardly fail to be a worldly success.

All this they see. What they fail to see is that the very work to which they have set their hands with so much resolution—the tribalization of the Puritan experience—is stifling its free spirit. Every repression of dissent, every insistence on the subordination of subjective experience to the judgment of the church, makes the work of enlisting zeal so much harder. They were probably right in thinking that order was possible on no other terms; but so was Anne Hutchinson when she accused them of substituting a covenant of works for a covenant of grace. Obedience to an external order, rather than immediate confrontation of God, was becoming, in spite of its formal theology, the criterion of New England Puritanism.

Before this first generation had passed away, it was obvious that the second generation would not be able to attest the conversion experience in sufficient numbers to perpetuate the succession of saints. It is some testimony to the severity of their standards that the fact was faced: that the second generation was held to be, and admitted itself to be, deficient in grace, though it was willing to support the church and to conform itself to its discipline. However, the sincerity of all parties only heightens the irony of a situation in which a chosen people cannot find enough chosen people to prolong its existence. Everything depended on saints. They composed the church and ruled the state. What would happen if the supply ran out? The escape was found through the famous halfway covenant, a device whereby the second generation was admitted to church membership, after making a profession of obedience, and so enabled to have its children baptized. The return to tradition had begun.[15] Of course the effort to produce conversions among the children and grandchildren was not abandoned. The preachers kept reminding themselves, and the clans, that the covenant had included Abraham's seed. But somehow, in spite of all their struggles, the religious experiences of the first generation refused to become a hereditary endowment. "Doth not a careless, remiss, flat, dry, cold, dead frame of spirit, grow in upon us secretly, strangely, prodigiously?"[16] We are hardly surprised to learn that the halfway covenant was in most cases just a halfway house between a church from which all but the saint had been excluded and one in which all but the flagrant sinner was admitted.

It was inevitable that this subsidence of the saints into a company of conformists should be reflected in the deterioration of Puritan piety. The congregations are not, of course, to be judged by the condemnations which the preachers heaped on them as part of the Puritan ritual during that prolonged jeremiad known to history as "God's controversy with New England." The deterioration is not a matter of crimes or misde meanors. It is entirely compatible with the most perse-vering virtues. But it means contracted sensibility; gestures replacing feelings; taste subduing zeal; pride elbowing out humility; intellect playing a game; divided souls acting a part their ancestors have forced on them. It is the well-meant mimicries of Samuel Sewall which produce such farcical effects when compared with the old, high seriousness. The diarist who finds it "an awful yet pleasing treat" to review the coffins in his family vault has traveled a long way from Bradford or Win-throp.[17] Equally far is the distance between the Puritan who knew the difference between spiritual and financial success and his descendant who sometimes confused them. The old Puritans had a grim description for this compromise with the covenant: they called it "the forms of godliness without the power."

Meanwhile, as a utopian church subsides into an established church, its grip over political power also relaxes. An early symptom was that pressure for a rule of law as opposed to a rule of discretion which distinguished the politics of Englishmen everywhere in the seventeenth century. Saints in power were always tempted to demand as free a hand for themselves as possible. A life-tenure for the trusted saint seemed to Cotton, as it later seemed to Milton, the best security for the holy commonwealth, and Winthrop's effort to keep a wide discretion in the hands of a chosen few has its counterpart in Cromwell's practice. But on both sides of the water the parliamentary tradition refused to be ousted by the theocrats. In Old England it was temporarily swept aside and then vindicated at the expense of the saints. In New England the saints discovered early that they would have to compromise with it if they hoped to control it. They were not even able to establish the system in Massachusetts without concessions to the principles of limited government which were extracted by the freemen in their struggles with the magistrates.

The intention, notwithstanding these concessions, was to maintain a theocracy within the forms of representative government, and the essence of the system was the restriction of political power to church members. In Massachusetts and New Haven this was achieved by confining the franchise to the elite. In Connecticut the same result could be expected without a formal restriction. But in the long run this monopoly of power was bound to be weakened by combined pressure from inside and outside: the pressure of expanding communities for a relaxation of religious tests and the pressure of imperial authority on a colonial theocracy. New Haven, the purest theocracy of the original settlements, had already suffered from its restrictive practices before its enforced absorption in Connecticut in 1662. Massachusetts, under pressure from England, went through the motions of liberalizing its religious tests at the same time. Finally, with the loss of the old charter in 1684, and the issue of a new one in 1691, the custodians of the Puritan ideal in Massachusetts were obliged to defend it under increasingly difficult conditions.

The power to choose their governor had passed to the Crown. Synods no longer advised legislatures. Boston flaunted the corruptions of a colonial court, the heresies of enforced toleration, and the sins of a thriving seaport before the eyes of the faithful, while the secularized culture of western Europe seeped in through a hundred different channels. No doubt all was far from lost. Preachers might keep their hold on rural communities by the combined force of personality and tradition. Conversions would certainly come back again; and the notion of a chosen people, still maintained in the pulpit, was only beginning its career in the world. But none of this should obscure the fact that an effort to escape from history into a utopia ruled by saints had suffered its usual failure.

✠ III ✠

Salvation through Separation

IT IS the thesis of this book that Puritans were elect
spirits, segregated from the mass of mankind by an
experience of conversion, fired by the sense that God was
using them to revolutionize human history, and committed to the execution of his Will. As such, they formed
a crusading force of immense energy; but it was an
energy which was incapable of united action, as the
elect souls formed very different conceptions of what
the Divine Will entailed for themselves, their churches,
and the unregenerate world outside the circle of the
saved. It was also an energy which everywhere sub-
sided from an ecstasy of zeal into standardized patterns
of behavior, as successive waves of enthusiasm were
broken on the resistant forces of human nature and as
men who had dreamed of a holy community found
themselves simply the administrators of a Puritan
tradition.

In my last chapter I dealt with one attempt to create
a framework of institutions within which the regeneration of fallen man—that miracle of rebirth within the
human soul which formed the grand object of all
Puritan striving—might go on indefinitely. That at-

tempt was the covenanted community erected in the wilderness by the founders of Plymouth, Massachusetts, New Haven, and Connecticut. In the covenanted community the basic principle was the conviction that the elect soul perceives in Scripture a form of worship appointed by God for man which church and state must sustain. All problems of conscience are resolved by a spiritual aristocracy, which applies its regenerate reason to the Word of God and enforces its findings on the community. Conversions, upon which the aristocracy depends for its renewal, though theoretically a matter of God's arbitrary pleasure, are expected to occur within the means offered by the church. The converted, if they are rightly instructed, will not challenge the orthodoxy which the church upholds. If they persist in erroneous opinions, the church will marshal its resources of grace and learning to produce repentance. If they do not repent, they will be proceeded against as blasphemers, idolators, schismatics, or heretics in accordance with the schedule of ecclesiastical errors. The state, which is simply the police department of the church, stands by to deal with them with the powers of punishment which can be brought to bear on the outward man: flogging, imprisonment, banishment, or execution. As for the unregenerate—that is to say, the majority of mankind who can obviously make no kind of claim to a work of grace in their souls—they will be protected in such civil rights as God intended them to have, exposed to the sermons which will save a few of them, and prevented from dishonoring the community by scandalous conduct.

This interpretation of the obligations and privileges of

the covenant between God and the elect soul was general throughout the Right and Center of the Puritan movement as Puritans passed from opposition into power. Though repellent to us, it ought to be appreciated in the context of a century-old tradition in which the societies of western Europe acknowledged a dogmatic commitment to the truths of Christianity. Working within that tradition, the first impulse of the Puritan saint was to erect a theocracy. But to attempt to do so was to try to seal off all the explosive possibilities of the conversion experience, and those who did so, either in New England or in Old England, found themselves confronted by a series of rebellions from saints who refused to be confined within the new orthodoxies. It is the purpose of this chapter to examine the extreme form which these rebellions assumed: the discovery that the saints' mission is to separate the church from the state. I shall first consider, in general terms, how the saints were led to this decision and what problems it created for them. I shall then examine Rhode Island as an attempt to fulfil the Puritan mission within the forms of religious freedom.

How does the Puritan saint convince himself that he must dissolve the church of tradition into a voluntary association and deny to the state any coercive power or positive duty in relation to religion? The development is complex; there are many different routes and many different degrees of separation. An early tendency in this direction is seen whenever the saint discovers that the church cannot be made to come up to his standards. The perfection that he seeks can be achieved only through withdrawal. The gulf that separates the regenerate soul from the natural man becomes absolute in his eyes, and any attempt to bridge it is a corruption. So, asserting the privileges of his new birth and aspiring to the purity which is only imaginable in a sect, he claims his liberty from both ecclesiastical and civil authority.

This impulse may have one of three results. First, it may carry him, as it carried the Anabaptists, into a complete repudiation of society and a search for absolute segregation within the crevices or on the frontiers of civilized life. Second, it may be arrested and stabilized in a theory of religious liberty: the saint proposes to live in society and to obey its laws, but he demands absolute freedom of worship. In the third contingency, the separatist becomes a militant millenarian, only withdrawing from the world in order to come back again with a sword in his hand. Both extremes—the retreat into a fortress for the pure and the militant return— had been vividly demonstrated when the mysteries of regeneration were first explored in Luther's day, and the prospects of a middle way were often to hang precariously balanced between the two.

A later tendency which reinforced these prospects, in certain situations, was the discovery that, as saints differed so much, no saint was likely to enjoy any liberty for his own conscience unless he was prepared to guarantee liberty to others. One is reminded of Voltaire's pleasantry: "If there had been in England only one religion, its despotism would have been fearful. If there had been two religions, they would have cut each other's throat. But as there are thirty, they live peacefully and happily."[1] This perception of the need for

toleration in a divided Christendom was often a re-
luctant discovery, but an agreement to live and let live
was bound to impose itself on some minds as a practical
necessity, and it could become a matter of principle
on the assumption that God had still much to reveal
and that his preferred method of revealing it was
through the free competition of prophecy. However,
though all separatists used these arguments, not all
who used them became separatists. They were arguments for varying degrees of toleration, and more was
needed than this to turn a tolerationist into the kind of
man who would insist that in religious belief the individual conscience was alone binding.

When one turns to the famous names among the
separatists thrown up by English Puritanism—Williams, Milton, Vane, Saltmarsh, Dell, the Quakers—
generalization is still difficult, as each structures his
opinions with the terms of his own piety. What is clear
is that all have passed through an intense religious
experience; that all recoil from the external discipline
which orthodox Puritanism tries to insert between the
regenerate conscience and God; that all combine an
acute sense of the uncertainty of human judgment in
the past with an abounding confidence in the revelation
that is going on around them; and that most of them are
either pronounced rationalists or pronounced mystics.
These two paths, rationalism and mysticism, are not the
only routes, but they are among the more obvious. If
the regenerate soul fastens on rationality as the essence
of God's revealed will, and on reason as the faculty
through which man, made in the image of God, is to
relate himself to his maker and his fellow-men, he is

liable to discover that the regenerate life is a life of free inquiry and free moral choice and to spend his whole pilgrimage trying to substitute self determination for submission to any outward law. This is what Christian liberty came to mean for Milton. It is a doctrine of conscience which embraces the idea of the individual as a church in himself and employs every resource of prophetic scorn against the notion that ecclesiastical or civil coercion can contribute anything to the growth of grace. Alternatively, the mystic, envisaging God as spirit and believing himself possessed by it, transcending all the means offered by the church in his mystic union, and protesting in both his noble and his lunatic moods the sovereign right of the spirit to free expression in this glorious age of testimony—who was more likely to reach the conclusion that church and state must be separated? A secure church can either contain its mystics or dismiss them into heresy. A church shattered by a chain reaction of spiritual energy invites replacement by mystics who claim for themselves exactly the same authority as the apostles. Such were the Quakers, and Quakerism was simply the end result of tendencies which are clearly seen in Vane, Saltmarsh, and Dell and which had led them to insist on separatism.

So much for the experience which is liable to turn a saint into a separatist: one, that is to say, who will demand complete freedom for the religious conscience from ecclesiastical or civil authority and who is willing to forego any claim by the godly to govern society.

What were his problems? His first problem was to convince everyone outside his own fraternity that he had a right to start his experiment. He was flouting the tradition of a thousand years, and everything about him seemed an outrage to right-minded people. Perhaps a start could be made on the frontier. But in England the experiment could be made only through revolution and military dictatorship. In that event two things happened. All separatists, except the Quakers, abandoned one half of their profession in order to enjoy the half which mattered more. They became theocrats in spite of themselves, because the liberty which they demanded for the religious conscience—the freedom to worship, to prophesy, and to dismantle, if they could, every remnant of an established church—could be enjoyed only if saints like themselves wielded a dictatorial power over the political community. At this point freedom for the regenerate has come to mean, once again, the coercion of the natural man: the kind of coercion which Cromwell practiced when he governed through military despotism, or which Vane and Milton were driven into. The other possibility has already been touched on. In the wild excitements of revolution many of the separatists became militant millenarians under the impression that the hour had struck for the saints to inherit the earth.

The second problem, assuming that the experiment could be begun without a revolution, was to demonstrate that the emancipated conscience was capable of submitting to any social discipline. Its critics were convinced it could not. It seemed to them, not without reason, to be the kind of anarchism which dissolved all obligations, and especially the obligation of the lower classes to stay in their places. It remained to be seen whether it would work on the frontier.

The third problem, if the other two were successfully solved, was to see if the Puritan impulse could conserve itself any better within the forms of religious freedom than elsewhere.

The colony of Rhode Island was not planned by anybody. It scratched and clambered into existence out of bands of fugitives and exiles who were either ejected out of Massachusetts or chose to try their fortune elsewhere. Its settlers included prophets and prophetesses; inspired tanners, tailors, and tapsters; disgruntled elders; characters like Captain Underhill, who enjoyed saying that after years of useless churchgoing he had found himself saved while smoking a pipe of tobacco; soldiers of fortune; and a lot of little people whose only object in life was to get themselves a bit of land and see how many other bits they could add to it. However, of the six personalities who dominated this little theater in the wilderness, four of them—Roger Williams, Anne Hutchinson, John Clark, and Samuel Gorton—were definitely prophets; a fifth, William Coddington, began his exile with a mosaic flourish; and the sixth, William Harris, found it entirely natural to enliven his real estate operations with an appeal to the sovereign rights of conscience.

To see the separatist thrust at work in some of these prophets, let me pause a moment over two of them: Roger Williams and Samuel Gorton.

In nine-tenths of his opinions Roger Williams saw eye to eye with the Cottons and Winthrops who banished him. Like them, he thought that salvation was all that mattered, believed in predestination, preached the new birth and the life of rigorous self-examination and self-denial that followed. The little treatise which he wrote for his wife's guidance, called *Experiments of Spiritual Life and Health*,[2] and the steadfast resistance which he put up during his impetuous pilgrimage to all the seductions of "honor, profit, and preferment" which beguile the unwary in this world would both command their approval. Like them, he treated Scripture as an absolute authority and used the same tools of learned analysis to expound it. Nor did he break with them because he had any quarrel with aristocracy as a principle of political government or any ambition to found a democratic community. He broke with them because he convinced himself, in a series of collisions with the Massachusetts authorities, that they were not taking sufficiently seriously the gulf which separates the regenerate from the unregenerate and that the covenanted community of the New England pattern was actually a horrible perversion of God's declared Will.

Williams' arguments, as they were developed in the course of a long controversy with orthodoxies in both New and Old England, are notoriously difficult to summarize. The main features, as they appear and reappear through the churnings of biblical polemic, are threefold. First, an exposition of New Testament texts, such as the parable of the wheat and the tares, to demonstrate that the most erroneous conscience imaginable is not to be disturbed in its errors by force; second, a ruthless disposal of all the Old Testament precedents by the device of "typology," which I shall explain shortly; and, third, a series of scattered but razor-sharp expositions of the nature of church and

state as utterly different societies. But all this is im-
bedded in very wearisome prose, and it is made more
complicated by the fact that he has absorbed many
other arguments which his predecessors had struck off
in the past century. Personally, I find him easiest to
understand when I fasten on three positions which he
offered to defend in public debate toward the end of his
stormy career. First, that forced worship stinks in
God's nostrils; second, that forced worship denies the
coming of Christ by insisting on the national church of
the Jews; third, that religious liberty is the only
prudent, Christian way of preserving peace in the
world.[3]

When Williams reflects on the history of the effort
to enforce religious orthodoxy, two impressions seem to
occur to him: such efforts misunderstand the church
(that is to say, they are incompatible with the nature of
those who profess to be elected) and they destroy the
civil peace which God has commanded for both the
elect and the natural man during their earthly pilgrimage. To the degree that the welfare of the church
transcends the welfare of natural man, the first consideration has the priority. The real sufferers from the
doctrine of forced worship have always been the saints.
It places them at the mercy of any error which clerical
authority may commit, as Williams himself had been
victimized by the Massachusetts hierarchy. It invites
the natural man, through his representative, the political government, to impose his ideas in a realm in which
he is absolutely unfit to have an opinion. It fosters the
delusion that the "garden of the church"—that hedged
inclosure for a few rare blooms—was ever intended to

embrace "the wilderness of the world." It obscures the true nature of conscience as a faculty which is bound to judge differently until the day when God chooses to enlighten it fully. The only escape from these monstrosities is to realize that regeneration is a spiritual process, to be promoted by purely spiritual means, including the unimpeded testimony of prophets through whom the spirit is speaking to this age.

But if forced worship stinks in God's nostrils, how is this to be reconciled with the first four of the Ten Commandments? Has the Gospel destroyed the law? New England had built its orthodoxy on those commandments. Puritans in Old England who discovered reasons for toleration had great difficulty in believing that a Christian magistrate had no duty under those commandments to repress false worship. Ireton was to speak for them on one occasion when he checked the appeal to Christ's ministry with the obvious retort: "It is not enough to show us what Christ preached: it is necessary to show us how the duty given to the magistrate under the Old Testament has been superceded under the New."[4] Williams got rid of this difficulty by a sweeping use of the device of typology which was frequently employed to relate the Old Testament to the New, but seldom as boldly as this. The construction placed upon these commandments by the Jews was not to be taken as a literal model by John Cotton or anybody else. It was to be understood as a symbol of the spiritual church of Christ, and to invoke it as a model for coercive institutions was in effect to deny the coming of Christ.[5]

So forced worship stinks because it is perverting

God's plan for the regeneration of souls. But it is also frustrating his command that the regenerate man and the natural man must live together in peace. The saint is not "of the world," but he must live in it, under a temporal regime of law which protects the civil rights of both the saved and the damned. But what security can mankind enjoy for their bodies and goods, what peace is possible during these centuries of religious warfare, so long as the world is trapped in the fallacies of forced worship? The agency for providing this security is the state, and the natural reason given by God to all mankind is the only guaranty we possess. Doubtless it is insufficient to prevent sin from committing its enormities, but it has sufficed to produce long periods of peace where the name of Christ was never heard of, and it will be made less, not more, sufficient by intruding the claims of the saints in a sphere where they do not belong. If they cannot advance Christ's kingdom by claiming earthly power, neither can they promote the peace of the world. God gave his saints no commission to rule the world, as we might guess, if no other reasons existed, from the fact that he chooses them from ranks which are rich in faith but poor in worldly skill.[6] So little have they in common with the men who have governed the world throughout its history! Yet, damned as the ruling classes almost certainly are, in Williams' estimate, it is still their business to rule.

It was in this spirit that Williams was prepared to generalize his case for what he called "soul liberty." Taken literally, it meant that the church would simply be a voluntary corporation within a secularized state and that churches, true and false, would have the same liberty. As such, it was one of the most breath-taking demands ever made.

Samuel Gorton, though a rich and redoubtable figure, need not detain us so long. Massachusetts, with that weakness for attributing gratuitous sins to its enemies, which was always a Puritan failing, was to accuse him of having run away from England to escape a debt. But there is no reason to doubt his own word that he came to enjoy the privileges of election, among them the privilege of prophecy. He arrived, however, in the midst of the Antinomian controversy, when prophets of his own stamp, like Anne Hutchinson, were being weeded out, so either for that reason or for some other he withdrew to Plymouth. There, however, after the first good impression which a godly man was bound to make, there began to be grave doubts about what they had welcomed. The new inhabitant, to use his favorite description of himself, was "a professor of the mysteries of Christ," with his own access to divine knowledge and alarming talents for conversion—talents so alarming that several citizens who had enjoyed the benefits of his parlor prophecies, including a minister's wife, began to make very unflattering comparisons between the official religion and the professor's. And so began the first of many brawls in which the professor, after giving a fine display of Divine knowledge, legal knowledge, and demagoguery, was naturally banished.[7] From his point of view he was the victim of a stacked decision by an intolerant court. From the colony's point of view he was a born troublemaker.

Whether Gorton was a troublemaker depends, of course, on the point of view. He had strong convictions about civil justice, which I shall return to. What he demanded in the way of religious freedom was the right to expound the mysteries of Christ as the spirit moved him, which meant in his case preaching a doctrine of mystical union between Christ and the regenerate, condemning all outward forms of worship, and reinterpreting the traditional teaching of the church on such matters as the Trinity or immortality to suit his fancy. He demanded a hearing for these opinions, which he considered were not his opinions but the Holy Ghost's; and, whenever he was whipped or banished, there was always some disciple standing by to cry, "Now Christ Jesus has suffered!" To molest him was certain to produce trouble, but what would happen if he ever found a place where he could enjoy the liberty he asked for?

The colony of Rhode Island eventually became such a place, with Gorton installed, after many adventures, as the founder of one of its four towns. The first of the separatist's three problems—the problem of persuading a community to make an experiment in soul liberty—was solved. This was due partly to the determination of prophets like Williams, Gorton, and Clark and partly to certain characteristics of these settlers which predisposed them to try such an experiment, the chief being the diversity of opinion among them which made an orthodoxy a practical impossibility, and the number of rebels against all clerical pretensions. The decision in favor of religious liberty was not made immediately by each community at the time of its migration; if Williams was committed to it when he founded Providence, the Antinomians were not committed to it when they founded Portsmouth and Newport. And after it became a rallying point for the common defense of the settlements against Massachusetts, there were plenty of second thoughts on the subject. There were elements, both in Providence and on the island, who would gladly have given up soul liberty for a little more social security and who were prepared either to submit themselves once again to Massachusetts or to carve out a more orthodox shelter for themselves. However, these elements were eventually defeated, and "soul liberty"— a liberty unique in the seventeenth century—became the distinguishing mark of Rhode Island.

The second problem for the separatist was to discover whether the emancipated religious conscience was capable of social discipline and, if so, what sort of discipline. What the religious separatist demanded was an area of freedom, "in matters of God's worship," within which, as he said, Christ was sole lord over the individual conscience. But how far did that area extend, and what human government was he prepared to obey outside that area? These were questions which separatists seldom faced while they were in opposition. They generally protested that they had no quarrel with the ordinary obligations of civil life, that all they wanted was their soul liberty, and that they would live gratefully under any government that gave it to them. But, as soul liberty came within reach, it soon became apparent that the questions would have to be faced and that no simple answer was going to be given to them.

If one surveys the history of separatists in different situations, one finds that their "soul liberty" can have at least four different consequences so far as the political order is concerned.

Puritanism in Old and New England

First, there is the possibility already mentioned—the separatist may become a militant millenarian. This happens only in revolutionary situations—of great hopes and great dangers—where saints are not quite sure whether they are going to be slaughtered or whether Christ is coming to rule the earth through them. This happened at Munster, and it happens in the English Revolution.

Second, "soul liberty" may lead to anarchism of one form or another. There is a story taken from the history of Antinomianism in England which describes the sort of people we are dealing with. It is told by a bitter enemy of the sects, but there is no reason to dismiss it as a freak of malicious fancy.

About the beginning of Lent last, Master Faucett, Minister of Walton upon the Thames in Surrey, preached in his parish church after dinner. When he came down out of his pulpit it was twilight; and into the church came six soldiers, one of them with a lantern in his hand and a candle burning in it; in the other hand he had four candles not lighted. He with the lantern called to the parishioners to stay a little, for he had a message to them from God; and offered to go up into the pulpit, but the parishioners would not let him; then he would have delivered his errand in the church, but there they would not hear him; so he went forth into the church-yard, the people following him, where he related to them;

That he had a vision and received a command from God to deliver his will unto them; which he was to deliver and they to receive upon pain of damnation. It consisted of five lights:

1. That the Sabbath was abolished as unnecessary, Jewish, and merely ceremonial. And here (quoth he) I should put out my first light, but the wind is so high I cannot light it.

2. Tythes are abolished as Jewish and ceremonial, a great burden to the Saints of God, and a discouragement of industry and tillage. And here I should put out my second light, etc., as aforesaid, which was the burden of his song.

3. Ministers are abolished as anti-Christian, and of no longer use now Christ himself descends into the hearts of his Saints, and his

Spirit enlighteneth them with revelations, and inspirations. And here I should have to put out my third light, etc.

4. Magistrates are abolished as useless, now that Christ himself is in purity of spirit come amongst us, and hath erected the Kingdom of the Saints upon earth; and beside they are tyrants and oppressors of the Liberty of the Saints, and tie them to laws and ordinances, mere human inventions. And here I should have put out, etc.

5. Then putting his hand into his pocket, and pulling out a little Bible, he showed it open to the people, saying, "Here is a book you have in great veneration, consisting of two parts, the Old and New Testament; I must tell you, it is abolished: It containeth beggarly rudiments, milk for Babes. But now Christ is in Glory amongst us, and imparts a fuller measure of his Spirit to his Saints, than this can afford; and therefore I am commanded to burn it before your faces." So, taking the Candle out of his lantern, he set fire to the leaves. And then putting out the candle, cried, "And here my fifth light is extinguished."[8]

This speaks for itself. The saint is capable of invoking his privileges to undermine all the obligations of social life. He may demand the right to sin in order to prove his superiority over sin. He will tell you that conduct which is sin in others is no sin in him. He may discover a conscientious objection to bearing office, paying taxes, or submitting to legal process. He may have suffered so much from authority that he thinks that society can get along without any. He will tell you that arbitration ought to replace government; that no law ought to be binding which is not approved by the individual conscience. This is a spirit which can be invoked to justify anything, and it results in conduct which ranges through different degrees of lawlessness from nonco-operation in trifles to a complete repudiation of authority.

Third, the separatist may become a constitutionalist. He wants his "soul liberty," but, if he can get that, he is prepared to accept the English constitution as he finds it. Because of his experience of arbitrary power and his alliance with parliamentarians, he thinks of it as a liberal constitution. But it is not a democratic constitution, and he has no ambition to democratize it. He simply wants the securities for property, for personal liberty, and for representative government by the classes with a stake in the country, which are upheld by the English common-law tradition. Magna Carta, symbolizing a rule of law under a limited monarchy, is good enough for him. He is not interested in a Declaration of the Rights of Man.

Finally, the separatist may become a doctrinaire democrat. He demands that the state should be organized on the same principles as his little church. His religious congregation has a voluntary covenant as its basis; saints are regarded as equals; they settle their problems by free discussion. So, by analogy, the state ought to have a social contract as its basis; its citizens ought to be considered equal; and government ought to approximate to direct democracy as closely as possible.

Given this variety of possible inferences from the separatist position, it is not surprising that contemporaries equated them with anarchists and that Massachusetts and her associates spent thirty or forty years trying to wipe out Rhode Island. However, Rhode Island did demonstrate that its settlers were capable of enough social discipline to form a little commonwealth, which was able to defend itself against both internal disorder and external aggression. Of the four possible inferences of which I have spoken, it is agreed that

Salvation through Separation

Rhode Island was not plagued by millenarianism of the violent variety. There is the millenarianism of the frustrated prophet who may feel in his own mind that the world is so wicked that God is bound to be coming to judge it soon; but there is no party with swords in their hands trying to seize power. That is a mood which thrives on persecution and which assails the saint when he is backed into a corner. But here it was always possible for Samuel Gorton to obey the apostolic injunction, "If they persecute you in one city, flee into another."[9] And when he had exhausted them all, he could build his own.

It has been suggested that the fourth line of development did occur—the line which turns the separatist into an advocate of the rights of man. And Roger Williams, in particular, has been hailed as the "Irrepressible Democrat": a champion of social democracy who gave the best efforts of his later years to the construction of a democratic republic and who fought a noble, losing struggle against the encroaching forces of colonial privilege.[10] But this is based on a misreading of his character and his writings. He was irrepressible enough, and noble enough, but it is the irrepressibility and the nobility of the passionate pilgrim who spends his life trying to save souls and to win for them the soul liberty they desire. He would have taken soul liberty gratefully from any government. He is content to enjoy it in Rhode Island either under the authority of Parliament, a Cromwellian dictatorship, or a restored Stuart. When he visits England in the course of the Revolution, it is the struggle for soul liberty that interests him, not the struggle for civil liberty. He has no contacts with the

Puritanism in Old and New England

Levellers, the only genuinely democratic party thrown up by Puritanism. When he has to concern himself in Rhode Island with the details of political organization—a task for which he had no particular talent—he shows himself to be a constitutionalist, trying to adapt English representative institutions to a frontier situation, but with no commitment to social democracy. The passages in his writings which are usually quoted as evidence of a faith in political equality turn out to be either a separatist's protest against clerical privilege or simply a Christian protest against greed.[11]

What Rhode Island actually experiences, in terms of my four alternatives, is the miscellaneous lawlessness of the second category which is gradually surmounted by the constitutionalism of the third. The result is a commonwealth which bears the marks of its original individualism for the next hundred years, in various habits of nonco-operation and obstructionism, but which offers no resistance to the emergence of a little colonial aristocracy built out of fortunes in land and trade and concentrating effective power in its own hands. William Coddington, one of these little aristocrats, spent years of his life trying to avoid having to live under the same government as Samuel Gorton, even if it meant taking the island back under the wing of Massachusetts or getting authority from England to govern it himself. But he might have spared himself the worry. Once Gorton had complete freedom to prophesy in a town of his own making and the privilege of being a magistrate under a constitution sanctioned by English authority and observing English common-law principles—he was always a great stickler for that—he gave no further trouble. Though the prophet continued to be a prophet, the born nuisance disappeared.

What of the last of the separatist's problems—the one he shares with all Puritans? Could he succeed, any better than they, in keeping the crusading energy alive?

However we may judge the experiment in Rhode Island, it is clear that a Williams or a Gorton would judge it by the progress of conversions, by the appearance of more and more prophets, and by the conviction that this haven for the persecuted would form a beacon for the whole world. Before he died in 1683, after one of the most strenuous and impetuous Puritan pilgrimages on record, Roger Williams had his own reasons for frustration. He had fought a lifelong battle with the proprietors of Providence to preserve that town as a public trust for religious refugees, only to see it turned into an investment company for the founding families. That defeat became a symbol of the future. In 1664 he wrote a letter to Winthrop's son: "Sir, when we that have been the eldest and are rotting [in our graves] a generation will act, I fear, far unlike the first Winthrops and their *Models of Christian Charity:* I fear that the common trinity of the world—Profit, Preferment, Pleasure—will be here the *tria omnia,* as in all the world besides: that Prelacy and Popery too will in this wilderness predominate; and that God Land will be as great a God with us English as God Gold was with the Spaniard."[12]

There were no more Puritan prophets to follow Williams and Gorton. Gorton left a few Gortonists behind him, but a sect which subsists on a personality is not going to last long. His theology is unintelligible. A disciple of Vane, another Puritan mystic who left a few Vanists behind him, said of his master, "He was a partaker of the Divine Nature (2 Pet. 1.4), t'is past the skill of humane nature to interpret him. . . . He had the *New Name*, which no man knowes but he that hath it."[13] The last disciple of Samuel Gorton sufficiently explained the disappearance of Gortonism when he said that his books "were written in Heaven, and no one could read and understand them unless he was in Heaven."[14]

Admittedly another race of prophets were to reap where the seekers and mystics had sowed. A community which stood fast by religious liberty, and which still contained many enthusiasts within its otherwise secularized membership, was ready to receive Quakerism. But Quakerism, the last eruption of spiritual lava from the seventeenth-century volcano, goes through the same cooling process of compromise and concession as Puritanism, and we may infer from the fact that William Coddington embraced it that its adaptation to the habits of prudent businessmen in the rising town of Newport was fairly swift. The Rhode Island which enters the eighteenth century has many sterling qualities, but from the point of view of its utopian founders it is a shell which has lost its kernel.

❧ IV ❧
Saints in Arms

IT WAS all very well for Puritans in a wilderness to
believe they were summoned to create a holy community, but in England no such hope could have sprung
if it had not been for the development of a secular revolution. It is in the midst of the struggles between king
and Parliament that the English saint discovers his
mission. The confused strivings became fused with
a providential purpose: a way is being opened for the
establishment of Zion. The revolution deepens. The
saints seize and dominate it. The grand iconoclasm,
sustained by the grand utopianism, grinds on until every
shred of established authority has been swept away.
But long before then the saints have discovered that
many of them are enemies or strangers to each other,
that they have been united in nothing but the will to
destroy, that the hero who embodies so much of their
aspiration is himself a puzzled pilgrim, and that the
enemies without are only waiting for the collapse within
to sweep the whole endeavor aside. A crusade shattered
by its own contradictions, a classic tragedy in the politics
of enthusiasm—this is what the Puritan thrust produces in its English setting.

The opportunity which the Puritan found in the
English situation was partly his own making. Since

Elizabethan days he had been agitating for the reform
of the church, contracting alliances, and learning the
tactics of parliamentary opposition, all of which
helped to produce the crisis in the relations between
king and Parliament. But the movement of resistance
to royal and episcopal authority, on which he was
going to impress the character of a religious crusade,
was nourished by factors which had nothing to do with
religious experience. What was this other half of the
story which lies behind the English rebellion of the
seventeenth century—the half which the older historians used to call the "constitutional movement," directed toward a larger degree of self-government, to
distinguish it from the Puritan half, directed toward
the reform of the church?

The opportunity for a constitutional conflict lay in
the fact that royal government in England had always
depended on the co-operation of the nobility and
gentry. The Tudor sovereigns had exalted royal power
in all sorts of ways; but they had not destroyed the
protection given by the common-law tradition to personal liberty and property, and they had increased the
importance of Parliament by deliberately developing
it for their own purposes. The aristocracy—both the old
aristocracy of family and the new aristocracy of wealth
—were therefore in a position to make their influence
felt if, for one reason or another, they grew dissatisfied
with paternal government. Broadly speaking, they
had two reasons for being dissatisfied. One of them was
royal misgovernment—a grotesque failure of leadership on the part of the first two Stuarts. But if this had
been the only factor, why was Elizabeth, with her

wonderful talent for politics, running into difficulties
before the Stuarts ever came to the throne? And why
was the rebellion, when it came, not just the old type
of rebellion—the aristocratic scrimmage for power
which may dislodge the sovereign but which never
dreams of abolishing the monarchy and still less the
House of Lords? Many contemporaries, after living
through the frightful experience of regicide and republic, puzzled over this question; and, of all the answers,
the most interesting to the modern mind is Harrington's. Power, he said, depends on property. Property
was once the monopoly of the few—a king surrounded
by a baronage—but it is now diffused among the many,
and our revolution is the inevitable result.[1] This interpretation caught the eye of eighteenth-century historians like Hume,[2] was somewhat submerged in the
nineteenth century, but then received a tremendous
boost in the twentieth century with the modern vogue
for economic interpretations. Professor Tawney is
Harrington in modern dress, and his concept of "the
rise of the gentry" has been widely accepted as the
fundamental explanation of the constitutional struggle.[3]
According to his thesis, the social changes of the sixteenth century had been weakening certain elements
in English society and strengthening others; the Crown,
the church, and the nobility had been losing ground,
while the gentry—an upper layer of commoners embracing the landed gentleman, the merchant, the in-
dustrialist, and the lawyer—had been gaining. Stuart
incompetence simply forced a showdown between the
king and the representatives of these classes in Parliament, with the issues ranging over the whole field of

government—personal liberty, security of property, freedom of enterprise, foreign policy, religious policy, control of the armed forces, and the choice of ministers. Each side protested that the other was the aggressor, and each engaged in innovations while pretending only to protect the constitution. The king, forced back onto emergency prerogatives if the government was to be carried on at all, gave some color of plausibility to the charge in the Grand Remonstrance that he was trying to replace a government of law by a government of arbitrary power. But the more serious innovator was actually the Parliament, for, whether it knew it or not, what it was really demanding was a transfer of sovereign power.

The old regime was brought to a standstill in 1640, after a long history of worsening relations in which each attempt to find a compromise had failed. For the eleven years before 1640, king and bishop had ruled without a Parliament. The price of this policy had been complete insignificance in Europe and mounting resentment in England, but it might have gone on for several years if an attempt to mold Puritan Scotland into the same pattern of docile Anglican obedience had not provoked a rebellion. It proved impossible for the king and his agents to restore this Scottish situation without summoning the English Parliament, and Parliament would do nothing without a change of system.

This constitutional movement has its own logic of development in the upheavals which follow, as its representatives have to make up their minds how far they are prepared to go. Its first impulse is to seek a compromise, through peaceful legislation, whereby the king will sacrifice some of his discretionary power without losing his independence. The most cautious reformers never go beyond this point and are prepared to fight for the king to arrest the revolution. These are the constitutional royalists. Others, because they distrust the king, are led to demand more than they originally planned and to fight him for a version of limited monarchy that would transfer effective sovereignty to Parliament; but many of them, after they have defeated him in one war, will be forced by their fear of further revolution into making concessions to him. Others, still thinking within the framework of limited monarchy, will experiment with written constitutions in which they try to prevent either the king or the Parliament from having too much power. Others will jump right out of the tradition of limited monarchy into dogmatic republicanism. Some of these will want an aristocratic republic; some will travel as far as the logic of liberty will take them and demand a democratic republic.

Each of these factions will have to decide what sort of church they want, because the starting point of the process is a community in which church and state are identical, and the bishop has been sustaining the king in a system of absolute government. In making their decision, individuals are affected by the seriousness with which they take the claims of the religious conscience, but in each faction there is a large group— perhaps a majority —whose only motive is political. That is to say, they are looking for the religious settlement which will best buttress the kind of liberty they want. Their choice of Anglicanism, Presbyterianism, or Congregationalism, and their attitude toward different degrees of toleration, are determined by a political calculation. Appropriately enough, a vigorous strain of anticlericalism runs through all of them, reflecting the determination of an increasingly lay society to put clerical leadership in its place.

It was in alliance with such forces as these that the Puritan crusade was launched. Naturally, it took time for the consciousness to develop and an infinite complication of circumstances before the constitutional movement was swept aside by militant crusaders. Doubtless hope sprang early. Cromwellian soldiers used to describe in later years how they were exceedingly stirred by the thought that the fall of the old regime was to be followed by the "dashing of the brats of Babylon against the wall."[4] But those soldiers were tending sheep in 1640, and the mood of the Long Parliament when it opened was anything but millenarian. Moderate Puritans like Pym had no desire to see the Puritan spirit get out of hand. More extreme Puritans like Cromwell and Vane were only extreme in demanding the abolition of episcopacy and very indignant at the suggestion that there might be any inconsistency between Christian liberty and the ordinary liberties of Englishmen. Many Puritans thought the interest of the church was only indirectly involved in the parliamentary debates; they took the Parliament's side because God was interested in civil justice, and this seemed to be primarily an argument about civil justice.[5] A few of them wondered if they had any business taking sides at all.[6]

Out of this situation a revolution develops which becomes progressively dominated by militant Puritanism. The search for a constitutional and religious compromise becomes a drift into civil war, with Parliament more or less pledged to the principle of a Puritan church. By the end of the first year of war any lingering hope of a compromise based on episcopacy has gone; peace negotiations have failed; and Parliament has pledged itself to impose a Puritan orthodoxy in order to secure the military assistance of the Scots. At the same time, Cromwell has begun to recruit Puritan enthusiasts to offset the military advantages which the royalists derive from their stronger hold on the privileged classes —a decision which may well be regarded as the turning point between a civil struggle and a religious crusade.[7] By 1645 the management of the war effort has passed into the hands of Cromwell and his friends, and the army which he has forged is a powerhouse of explosive energy. By 1646 the king has been decisively defeated, and all that remains is to see whether the Parliament which has unleashed such forces can possibly control them.

I propose to pause here, in the confused aftermath of the first Civil War, to take stock of the Puritan factions. What did the saints demand? At least four programs can be distinguished, and each may be viewed as an effort to make the settlement fit the aspirations of the Puritan conscience.

On the Right of the movement were the Presbyterians. They have an ancestry which goes back to the efforts of Elizabethan Puritans like Cartwright and Travers to bring the Church of England in line with the best reformed churches. Their standard is the Word of

God. What they find in the Word of God, in addition to the usual Puritan theology and ethics, is a command to erect a Presbyterian church, as the ecclesiastical order through which souls are saved and the community disciplined. Such a church will embrace the whole community: it has this in common with the church of tradition. But the full privileges of church membership—the power to determine truth and error and to control the access to the communion table —will be reserved for an aristocracy of grace. Ideally speaking, the elect should dominate the whole government of society. The Presbyterian impulse finds its fullest satisfaction in Calvin's Geneva, in John Knox's Scotland, or in the covenanted community of New England, if the New Englanders would only realize that God is not a Congregationalist but a Presbyterian. In each case the drive is to reduce the state to a police department of the church. However, this can happen only when the church is established, and the job in this English situation is to get it established. The English Presbyterian has to make the best of his circumstances, uphold the authority which seems most likely to do its Christian duty, and use whatever un-Christian allies the Lord throws in his path.

During the first Civil War he upholds the Parliament and justifies its resistance with arguments which would quite easily extend to deposing the king, if the only obstacle to the erection of a Presbyterian church were an obstinate monarch. But toward the end of that war he is filled with so much fear and horror by the heresy and subversion which is tearing through the Puritan movement that his one object is to clinch some sort of deal between the Parliament and the king which will give his church some stamp of approval and seal off the Revolution. Ideally, the king should take the Covenant; but, if Charles I refuses, there are Presbyterians who will settle for a promise that he will give Presbyterianism a three-year trial. Ideally, Parliament should take the Presbyterian divine a good deal more seriously than it does; but a Presbyterian church botched by unregenerate members of Parliament who are backing it as the safest bet after they have taken some of the theocratic sting out of it is vastly preferable to letting the Independent Army dictate a solution.

It should not surprise us that the average income of the faction calling itself Presbyterian was appreciably higher than that of any other section of the Puritan movement. No doubt that was partly due to the fact that many people calling themselves Presbyterians at this time were not Puritans at all in any real sense. They were simply peers who had discovered they were on the wrong side and were trying to make the best of a bad business, or well-to-do gentry who found Presbyterianism a useful counterpart to Parliament's claims. It is also emphatically clear that anyone who tries to correlate the movements of the Holy Spirit with the incomes of the regenerate is in for a lot of headaches. However, there seems to have been a certain tendency for a converted soul with £1,000 a year to feel anxieties which troubled Oliver Cromwell somewhat less and several of his captains not at all. Men of rank and family, owners of wide acres, and directors of big business clung to the protection of a church which upheld the ideal of a learned clergy against the vagaries of the illuminated spirit, possessed adequate organs of authority, and could be relied on to resist either the democratic or the millenarian inferences which could be drawn from the conversion experience.

Between this Puritanism of the Right and the programs of the Left is a composite Center party, the Independents. Initially, all that distinguished their clerical spokesmen from the Presbyterians was the discovery that Congregationalism, not Presbyterianism, was the form of church government appointed by God for his saints. A truly reformed church would consist of a loose federation of congregations, each a little aristocracy of grace, separated from the unconverted, and all preaching the same truths. If the powers that be understood their duty, they would erect such a church and protect it. Transplanted to New England, where the powers that be were themselves Congregational saints, this idea became the basis for an orthodoxy. In England its history was necessarily different. Forced to reckon with royalists and infidels in the seats of power, outnumbered by Presbyterians in the Puritan community, deprived of any means of disciplining themselves into agreement, exposed to all the winds of doctrine and enthusiasm to the left of them—the English Independent developed a need and a capacity for toleration which scandalized his New England brethren. Some of them, like Vane and Milton, were eventually to follow the trail blazed by Roger Williams and convince themselves that under the Gospel the state had no responsibility for the church beyond its duty to free it. Most of them were unable to make this break. But within certain limitations, which varied with the individual, they discovered the usual reasons why the regenerate conscience should enjoy liberty. The Will of God was not so clear that anyone could claim infallible knowledge. Truth, obscured by so much error, must be recovered by free inquiry or by the unimpeded ministry of the spirit whether it speaks through the learned or the unlearned. The Revolution has not been fought to replace an Anglican tyranny with a Presbyterian tyranny.

How far the Independent felt himself involved in the struggle for civil liberty varied with the individual. John Owen, a divine whom Cromwell was to make chancellor of the University of Oxford, was typical of those Puritans whose interest in the welfare of the church dwarfed all other considerations. "Give me leave to say, it is not for this or that form of government or civil administration of human affairs . . . that God hath wrought his mighty works amongst us; but it is *that Zion may be founded*, and the general interest of all the sons and daughters of Zion be preserved."[8] Ireton, on the other hand, while as interested as Owen in religious liberty for the saints, was equally interested in solving those problems of political sovereignty out of which the Revolution, in his opinion, had really sprung.[9] For him, as for Cromwell himself, the defeat of the king ought to have been followed by a settlement which combined liberty of conscience with securities for a rule of law, as opposed to a rule of royal discretion. Like the Presbyterians, they were thinking in terms of limited monarchy. But what would happen when the Presbyterians exerted themselves to produce a Presbyterian settlement? The Presbyterian stronghold was the

Parliament. The Independent stronghold was the Army. Would Cromwell submit to this dictation? Could he stop the Army from mutiny if he wanted to? And, once the mutiny started, where would it stop? One half of the Independent's nature shrinks from the anarchy which this prospect opens up. But the other half impels him to smite the saints' enemies and to consider prudence foolishness in these extraordinary times when God is shaking the kingdoms of the world. In this spirit, seeking the Divine Will in his labyrinth of confusion, the Independent can be led to purge the Parliament and execute the king, persuading himself that through this destruction he will enter his promised land.

To the Left of the Independents is the lower-class radicalism of the Puritan movement, inflamed by the breakdown of authority, by the incessant talk of liberty, by the opportunities which thrust the butcher, the carter, and the cobbler into positions of power, and by the wild debaucheries of the illiterate mind in the depths of Scripture. In this atmosphere all things are possible, as a conservative Puritan like Baxter discovered to his horror when he visited the Army after the victory at Naseby:[10] almost every heresy known to Christianity and almost every dream of perfection which has ever unbalanced the secular mind. Typically enough, the two discernible programs which emerge from this welter of emotion are absolutely unlike each other: a demand for a democratic republic based on a doctrine of equality and a demand for a dictatorship of saints based on the prophetic books of the Bible.

The first of these two programs was the work of the

Levellers—the only genuinely democratic party thrown up by the whole Puritan movement. It was so untypical for a Puritan to surrender himself to a political dogma that one wonders if this faction did not cease to be saints in the course of becoming democrats. But they began as saints and drew on the support of saints, and, if some of them were to drift far from their Puritan beginnings, others were to retreat into pietism after the political crusade was shattered.

Their leaders began their careers as separatists: converted souls who had withdrawn from the national church into the forbidden freedoms of the sect. These little cells attracted the rebel against society as well as the spiritual pilgrim, and they turned some spiritual pilgrims into social radicals. Their members lived double lives. In their ordinary occupations they were under the discipline of society with its hierarchy of classes and values; as worshipers, they escaped from it, admitting no superior but God, and managing their affairs as a community of equals in defiance of all custom and authority.

When the Civil War broke out, they joined the fight, some as civilians in London, many more as those men with the spirit of God in them on whom Cromwell pinned his hopes of victory. What were they fighting against? The spiritual tyranny upheld by the old regime or the social tyranny of courtiers, peers, landlords, merchants, lawyers, clergy? It was hard to tell. The first question they had to face was the shape of the future ecclesiastical settlement, as it became apparent, while the war was still on, that Parliament was moving in a Presbyterian direction. Here they came out as clear-cut separatists—the state must give the church its freedom—and, in making this demand, they are keeping company both with Roger Williams, whose only vital interest is in soul liberty, and with millenarians, who will demand soul liberty first and then persuade themselves that the saints must rule the earth. It is only in the postwar situation that the Leveller discovers himself as a man who is determined to combine the separation of church and state with a radical reconstruction of the state on democratic principles. Confronted by a Presbyterian-dominated Parliament which is bent on religious uniformity, which wants a change of masters at the top of society but no new deal below, the Leveller makes his radical leap. He appeals from Parliament to the people. To appeal to the people as the source of political authority was no novelty. What was novel was the idea that the people could govern themselves, without benefit from king, peers, clerical specialists, legal specialists, or any other kind of specialist in blood, property, or experience. The Leveller appealed to people whom God had created free and equal, who were entitled to government by consent, who had enjoyed some such freedom in a golden age before the Norman Conquest, and who should now seize their opportunity to vindicate their natural rights through a new constitution.

The Leveller's program, when examined by any disenchanted eye, must have seemed fatuous to the last degree. The idea that a profoundly hierarchical society could be turned into some equalitarian utopia was almost as grotesque an aberration as the idea that the second coming was at hand. He also quickly be-

came objectionable to Puritans who might be en-
chanted in other ways but not in this way; to Independents like Cromwell and Ireton, who saw that this
sort of appeal to natural rights could dissolve the whole
social order; or to Milton when he remembered that the
mass of the people were an unregenerate rabble. But,
if the Leveller's moment in history was brief, he made
the most of it. He caught up the resentments and
aspirations of a lot of little people, dramatized himself
and them, and opened a wonderful door of hope as the
reward for all their strivings. He did this to such effect
in the ranks of the revolutionary Army that for a time
he turned the high command into a debating society
where Levellers sat down with commanding officers to
discuss the rights of man. There came a day when the
hard-pressed Cromwell thumped the table as he sat
among his officers and cried, "I tell you, sir, you have
no other way to deal with these men but to break them,
or they will break you."[11] And broken they were. But
the mourners who filled the London streets for a Leveller's funeral,[12] or the London jury that acquitted a Leveller leader years later when he defied the Cromwellian
government,[13] were moving tributes to some of the
greatness of soul which had gone into a hopeless cause.

The Levelling program, in its own way, was one kind
of millenarianism—the kind that believes that an
earthly utopia is just around the corner. But side by
side with them, and close enough for individuals to
drift from one intoxication to the other, was the
millenarianism of the saint who remembers only too
vividly that his commission is not to build a democratic
commonwealth but to care for the church and that a

day has been promised when the suffering saints shall inherit the earth and rule it with or for Christ. Here we see how the separatist congregation, which the Leveller separates from the state, and then uses, either consciously or unconsciously, as a model for the construction of a democratic state, becomes for the millenarian a center of power which is going to engulf the state.

The first upsurge of this spirit may be traced to the breakdown of the old regime. One can easily imagine the effect on despised and persecuted outcasts of the events of 1641: the king on the defensive; Strafford executed; bishops mobbed on the streets; the Catholic queen fearful for her life; the Star Chamber abolished; silenced preachers back in their pulpits; everywhere a sublime smashing of idolatry, yet the work only half begun, and everywhere enemies plotting to undo it. Constitutional critics of the king like Edward Hyde saw enough anarchy in this prospect to decide him that trusting the king was a lesser evil than trusting the leadership of Pym and Hampden. Perhaps, among his many other reasons for being alarmed, he had read a sermon of that year entitled "A Glimpse of Zion's Glory." The text is Rev. 19:6: "And I heard as it were the voice of a great multitude, and as the voice of many waters, and as the voice of mighty thunderings, saying: Hallelujah, for the Lord God Omnipotent reigneth." The preacher, after reading the prophecies which had fired imaginations like his, in situations like his, for over a thousand years, chants to his rapt listeners: "It is the work of the day to cry down Babylon, that it may fall more and more; and it is the work of the day to give God no rest till he sets up Jerusalem as the praise of the whole world. Blessed is he that dasheth the brats of Babylon against the stones. . . . And beautiful likewise are the feet of them that bring glad tidings unto Jerusalem, unto Zion saying, The Lord God Omnipotent reigneth." He then asks, "From whence came this hallelujah?" and replies, "The voice, of Jesus Christ reigning in his Church, comes first from the multitude, the common people. The voice is heard from them first, before it is heard from any others. God uses the common people . . . to proclaim that the Lord God Omnipotent reigneth. As when Christ came at first the poor receive[d] the gospel—not many wise, not many noble, not many rich, but the poor—so in the reformation of religion, after Antichrist began to be discovered, it was the common people that first came to look after Christ. . . . You that are of the meaner rank, common people, be not discouraged; for God intends to make use of the common people in the great work of proclaiming the kingdom of his Son."[14]

Millenarianism, in one form or another, was not confined to the common people. It lifts the hearts and bedevils the politics of the Center as well as the Left of the Puritan movement. Milton, Vane, Owen, Cromwell—all feel its spell. But in the form in which it hardened into a faction, which maintains the same sort of demand for the next fifteen years, and which flings itself in a final contortion of despair against the restored government of Charles II, it was hardly calculated to commend itself to anyone above the social experience of Colonel Thomas Harrison or Colonel Goffe. Stripped of its rhapsodies of love, fear, hatred, and pity, its dark arithmetic about the date of the millennium and its speculations on the deeper mysteries of that glorious era, what it boiled down to was the simple proposition that the saints should seize power. It was not in its nature to worry unduly about how it was seized or how it was organized. Colonel Thomas Harrison was always confident that any group of saints which included himself would do very well. If the size of the group was a problem, seventy was a sanctified number, as that had been the size of the Jewish Sanhedrin. If it meant splitting the country into military districts and putting a saint over each of them, that would do too. Meanwhile, the great thing was to gather the saints and proclaim their mission. One proclamation which reached the commander-in-chief is a reminder that some logical training lingered in the most rhapsodical Puritan. He had heard his preacher subdivide his sermon too often not to be able to subdivide his own poem. Seven "Queries" are propounded and resolved as follows: "(1) There is a kingdom and dominion which the Church is to exercise on the earth. (2) That extends to all persons and things universally, which is to be externally and visibly administered, (3) by such laws and officers as Jesus Christ our Mediator hath appointed in his kingdom. (4) It shall put down all worldly rule and authority . . . ; (5) and is to be expected about this time we live in. (6) This kingdom shall not be erected by human power and authority, but Christ by his Spirit shall call and gather a people . . . and when they are multiplied, (7) they shall rule the world by general assemblies, or church-parliaments, of such officers of Christ . . . as they shall choose and delegate; which they shall do till Christ come in person."[15]

Here, at the close of the first Civil War, I shall leave the saints in arms—four groups of Puritans, each nursing its own idea of a holy community, surrounded by other factions who have been fighting only for constitutional liberty and confronted by a king who is determined to exploit these divisions. The common sense of the situation demands a negotiated settlement. But we shall see how the saints seize power, sweep aside the established institutions, and embark on a hopeless attempt to erect a holy community by force.

V

The Bankrupt Crusade

THE seizure of power came in the winter of 1648–
49, when the Puritan Army purged the Parliament,
executed the king, and abolished both the monarchy
and the House of Lords. That catastrophic decision was
not reached by following any master-plan. It was the
act of men who combined to destroy something without
any clear idea of what was going to take its place. It
reminds us, if we need any reminder, that a movement
like this English Revolution is an immense, inscrutable
disorder in which a bewildered people lurches from crisis
to crisis until all but the infatuated are ready to admit
they have lost their way.

The conditions for a successful compromise at the
close of the first Civil War are not difficult to stipulate.
First, it would have to be based on monarchy. In view
of the nature of society, this was the inevitable system
of the age, and there was little disposition among
Englishmen to believe that the special conditions which
justified a few aberrations on the Continent applied
to their island. The high aristocracy depended on monarchy for their own greatness. The gentry looked to the
court for privileges and the opportunities of service.
The City did business under its charters. The lawyer
found the kingship woven into every branch of the law

and shrank with horror from the surgery involved in removing it. The instinctive conservatism of the great mass of the community indorsed an institution which symbolized their unity, their national greatness, and their acceptance of the principle of inequality in human affairs. All this was properly signified by the theory— or, if you like, the prudent sophistry—of the first Civil War. By every practical test, that was a rebellion; but, by every profession of the rebels, it was a war undertaken in the king's name against a conspiracy of evil counselors around him. As the Earl of Manchester said to Cromwell, when that impatient warrior was chafing under his command, "If we beat the King ninety-nine times, yet he is King still, and so will his posterity be after him."[1]

Second, if based on monarchy, it would have to be limited monarchy. Some Englishmen, like Strafford and Laud, had allowed themselves, in their despair with the obstructionism and factionalism of the English Parliament, to cast some sidelong glances at the type of monarchy which was emerging on the Continent as the model of enlightened energy. But the future of England lay neither with Strafford and his paternal monarchy nor with the saints and their holy community but with the national tradition of mixed and limited monarchy with its ancient stock of precedents and its new sources of social strength. There should be kings in England, but kings ruling over a free people; and by freedom what was meant was security for personal liberty, for property, for due process of law, and for the right of the classes with a stake in the country to a say in the determination of policy. Such was the almost unanimous mood of the Long Parliament in its first session of 1641, when it obliged Charles I to relinquish his discretionary power to tax, to try cases in executive courts, and to do without Parliament. And such, after twenty years of devastating turmoil, was the unanimous mood of the Parliament of 1660 which invited Charles II to rescue them from a bankrupt revolution.

Third, the compromise would have to embody some agreement to live and let live in matters of religious belief. A national Anglican Establishment, upholding the principle of social unity, consecrating the legitimate ends of the state, and prudently linked with its structure, was demanded by every consideration of practical wisdom. But so also was some acknowledgment of what Burke once described as "the dissidence of dissent and the Protestantism of the Protestant Religion."[2] The proposals for "comprehension," which would have broadened the character of the Establishment to accommodate some Puritan scruples, offered one line of approach. The proposals for toleration, which would have allowed the unreconciled some freedom outside the church, offered another.

These three conditions for a successful compromise are easily enough stipulated. But there were three formidable obstacles to them. One was the king, who interpreted every proposal as a demand for the betrayal of his prerogatives, his church, and his friends and who saw in the divisions among his victors an opportunity for playing off one against the other. The second lay in the Presbyterians, both English and Scottish, who saw no security in anything but a Presbyterian victory.

The Bankrupt Crusade

And the third lay within the Army, where the demand for liberty of conscience was the opening wedge for as many different attacks on established institutions as the saint felt himself called to undertake.

Officially, the English Parliament and the Scottish commissioners were trying to get the defeated king to accept a treaty. Actually, each faction was maneuvering for power, and, with armies in the field, another appeal to force was only a matter of time if reason could not make itself heard above sectional strife. The first eruption of violence came in 1647, when the English Presbyterians tried to exploit their parliamentary advantage by disbanding the Independent Army, only to bring a mutiny on themselves. From that date the Army, organized as a political force, begins to dominate the Revolution. Its high command, represented by Cromwell and Ireton, continued to work for a treaty with the king, but the chances worsened as he continued to stall and as radical pressures built up within the Puritan Center and Left. The next eruption of violence followed the news that a deal had been made between the king and the Scottish commissioners, whereby he was given an Army in return for a dubious promise to experiment with Presbyterianism. So we have a second Civil War in 1648, in which a combination of royalists and Presbyterians tried to arrest the Revolution by defeating the Cromwellian Army, only to be defeated in turn.

We now reach the decision which was fatal to any chance of permanent settlement. Up to this point the English Parliament, though pressured by the Army, had not been purged. The common sense of the situa-

tion lay in resuming the search for a negotiated settlement with a king who was now in no condition to start
another war. This was what the Parliament, with its
Presbyterian majority, was anxious to do. This was
what the Independent minority in Parliament could
have joined them in doing, using the Army as a counter-
weight to restrain Presbyterian excesses. Some such
view had been Cromwell's own line when he warned the
Army, only a year before, "What we and they gain
in a free way, it is better than twice so much in a forced,
and will be more truly ours and our posterity's."[3] But
in those months the Holy Spirit had personally inter-
vened in the counsels of the Army, and common sense
was overruled.

The decision to purge the Parliament, kill the king,
and abolish the monarchy was defended in more ways
than one. It could be defended on the secular side of
the struggle by classical republicans who made a virtue
out of tyrannicide. It could be defended by Puritans
on the ground that Presbyterians were willing to
betray the Revolution for a scrap of paper signed by the
king,[4] though how that could happen while the Independents controlled the Army it is a little difficult to
see. Actually, for Cromwell and most of the Puritan
regicides, the decision was fanatical. It was the act of
the Puritan in his capacity as the executioner of Divine
justice.[5] It was reached through his method of prayer,
soul-searching, tears, and repentance, in which he
sought the Lord's face and found a blessing for his
violence. The Army had held a three-day prayer meeting before it broke camp to deal with the second Civil
War. As the warrior faced these new trials, after fight-

ing one war and finding himself no nearer the righteous man's deserts, he said to himself that this second war would never have been sent to scourge him if he had not grievously sinned. How had he sinned? How, indeed, if not by compromising with a man of sin—by trying to negotiate a settlement with an enemy of God, marked out for destruction.[6] Once this Divine persuasion had settled on the mind of the saint in arms, it mattered little if nine Englishmen out of ten regarded the regicide as an utterly criminal act. On the contrary, it braced him. The elect never felt more securely elected than when God upheld a few choice souls against the rage of a hardened multitude.

Doubtless the mind of Cromwell offered more resistance to iconoclasm than the minds of most of his saints. Macaulay was unwilling to believe that the greatest practical statesman of his generation could have failed to see that the regicide was a mistake. It must, he says, have been one of those situations in which the man who would lead is obliged to follow; he could keep control of the Army on no other terms.[7] But the mystic in Cromwell naturally eludes Macaulay. How should a good Whig, who never cultivated any piety except the religion of sensible men, understand a regenerate soul? "Perceiving," said Cromwell on another occasion when the Divine summons swamped his hesitations, "the Spirit of God so strong upon me, I would not consult flesh and blood."[8] He wrote a letter to his cousin, Robert Hammond, in the midst of this crisis, which throws some light on his method of reaching decisions.[9] The effort, of course, is to discover the Will of God. He begins by reviewing the arguments for purging the

Parliament which might appeal to the ordinary conscience, finds them less than conclusive, and moves on
to another plane. These, after all, were carnal arguments—the sort that might occur to the natural man—
the sort that could never carry the certainty which
springs from the immediate experience of the saint as
he consults the providences of God and follows the lead
of the spirit. So, following the lead of the spirit, without claiming to know where it is leading him, he puts
himself at the head of a movement which he has resisted for months and drives it through.

From now on, power is in the hands of the godly. For
three years the Army works with the fag end of a
House of Commons which it has been persuaded to
leave in being, while it destroys its enemies. It then
receives all the infallible testimonies of a Divine call to
destroy the Parliament, for the usual reason that these
sinful spirits are not the men to perfect the work which
God has begun. Cromwell goes through the same sort
of cycle as before: first the impulse to conciliate, the
effort to bring Parliament and Army together on some
agreed plan for a settlement. This is the Cromwell who
cries, in the midst of every crisis, "I am hugely taken
with the word *Settlement*."[10] Then comes the rising anger as the factions refuse to agree. And, finally, the
act of righteous violence, when he goes down to the
House with a file of musketeers and dissolves the
Parliament. This is the Cromwell who looks at the
mace, the emblem of civil authority, while the soldiers
are locking up the empty House, and asks, "What shall
we do with this bauble?"

This was in April, 1653. From then until his death

in September, 1658, he struggles to produce the settlement which his own acts have helped to make impossible. He is irresistible but purely provisional; without a rival but also without a future.[11]

This interlude in which the saints ruled England can be admired from several points of view. Considered as an achievement of national power, it lifted England to the heights which only a successful revolutionary regime, directed by able men, could be expected to reach. Suspended claims, dormant claims, claims only half-expressed, became realities as fast as the power developed to enforce them. By the time the saints laid down their arms, they had unified the British Isles for the first time in history and pushed its authority into every quarter of the globe. Considered as an example of dictatorship, it had some refreshing features compared with those we have known in our present century. If it shares with them the nightmare of enemies inside and outside, the secret police, the preventive arrests, and the endless purges, it also has its compensations. One was the guaranty of liberty of worship for all peaceable Christians. Another was the effort to impress standards of responsibility on all holders of office. A third was the handsome compliment which it paid to the English tradition by its recurring sense of guilt. Few dictators have shown so much reluctance for their role as Oliver, so much anxiety to get something tolerable done by consent instead of falling back on force. Finally, it put up with an amount of criticism which only a Puritan like Oliver would have tolerated. If England had to be governed by saints with swords in their hands, it was a great mercy to know that the commanding saint thought of himself only as a seeker after Divine truth and not as someone who had found it. He commits some violent acts while he is looking for it, but, in the long run, the tyranny of his theocracy is always tempered by humility, magnanimity, and common sense.

However, to pay these or any other compliments to the Cromwellian regime is to forget about the aims of the Puritan movement. Its real aim was to produce a holy community, and, as such, it is time to remind ourselves that the rule of the saints was a prodigy of stultification.

The first source of frustration was the unappeasable hostility of the mass of humanity. The attitude of the elect to the unregenerate was ambiguous. In one mood he believed that the relations between them were bound to be those of enmity, and the sort of hatred he aroused gave a relish to his existence. But, on the whole, this was the mood for moments of high excitement or for saints who had surrendered themselves to a state of perpetual excitement. More often he seems to have expected the unregenerate to appreciate what the saint was doing for him. Or perhaps one should say that he hoped, by an enormous dead lift of which only the Puritan was capable, to carry all the English sinners into a covenanted community where the natural man accepted the ideal of the elect and enjoyed such rights as God intended him to have.

Such was certainly the normal impulse of Independents like Cromwell. Though he was capable of scorning the idea of civil liberty in comparison with the benefits of godly government, and of ruling, if need be, through a military despotism, he always protested that there was no incompatability between the two goals for which the Revolution had been fought—Christian liberty and civil liberty—and half the experiments of his Protectorate were efforts to launch a written constitution under which liberty of conscience and a rule of law would be combined. But any chance of reconciling the two goals vanished when he abolished the monarchy. His constitutions, however well meant, reached the people from the hands of a conqueror who had to build his own power into each of them and who could trust none of their fundamentals to a free vote. Apart from security for property, the only freedom which he was able to offer the natural man was the freedom to co-operate with the saints, under conditions which the saints defined. Needless to say, a nation which had rebelled against Charles I, who could plead a good deal of custom for the king's right to dictate conditions, was not prepared to accept them from a group of self-certified saints. Looked at from a cynical point of view, the Cromwellian regimes were a dictatorship of lesser gentry and self-made soldiers who had seized power and were determined to hog its privileges. Looked at from a more charitable point of view, they were Puritan crusaders who had blundered into power and were then determined to subordinate the claims of the community to the welfare of a spiritual aristocracy. Whichever way you looked at it, it could only seem tyranny to the natural man.

This failure to make the natural man understand his blessings was one source of frustration, and it would be a mistake to underrate its impression on Cromwell.

However, a far greater source was the state of affairs among the communion of saints. The promises about the natural man were at best uncertain. But was it ever expected that the saints should become strangers and enemies to each other? The truth of the matter is that the movement was torn into fragments both by the variety of dogmatic inference which was possible to a Puritan when he was thinking about nothing but his religious experience and by the irregular incidence of social position and interest which tended to turn the well-heeled saint into a conservative and the under-privileged into a radical. The seizure of power naturally brought them no nearer the Promised Land. It simply left them wandering in the wilderness of their own discontents.

Listen to John Owen. Shortly after the regicide he had delivered a sermon called "The Shaking and Translating of Heaven and Earth," which ended with this peal of enthusiasm: "Is it not in vain to fight against the Lord? Some are angry, some troubled, some in the dark, some full of revenge; but the truth is, whether they will hear or forbear, Babylon shall fall, and all the glory of the earth be stained, and the kingdoms become the kingdoms of our Lord Jesus Christ."[12]

Listen to him in 1652—three years later, in another sermon:

What now, by the lusts of men, is the state of things? Say some, There is no gospel at all; say others, If there be, you have nothing to do with it;—some say, Lo, here is Christ; others, Lo, there:—some make religion a colour for one thing; some for another;—say some, The magistrate must not support the gospel; say others, The gospel must subvert the magistrate. . . . If you will have the gospel, say some, down with the ministers of it . . . and if you will have light, take care that you may have ignorance and darkness. . . . Now, those that ponder these things, their spirits are grieved in the midst of their bodies;—the visions of their heads trouble them. They looked for other things from them that professed Christ; but the summer is ended, and the harvest is past, and we are not refreshed.[13]

It was Cromwell's achievement to impose some sort of unity on this unruly flock and to sustain its sense of mission; but just how punishing the experience was may be gathered from what the saints had to say about the man who embodied so much of their aspiration. Each purge added its quota to the storm of indignation which was going to envelop him. First the Presbyterians, then the Levellers, then the Millenarians, then the Republicans, and, finally, every Puritan who revolted from the spectacle of the man who had abolished monarchy trying to restore it in his own person. He is being forced back on the old forms of government by the simple impossibility of governing England on any other terms, but, in the eyes of the greater part of the movement, he has sacrificed the cause to selfish ambition. The Puritan was always obsessed by his sense of sin. Taught to expect it everywhere, and to magnify it where he found it, he easily fell into the habit of inventing it. Every thwarted enthusiast, every purged idealist, is convinced that Cromwell has sold himself to the Devil. Here is a Leveller's opinion: "That grand impostor, that loathsome hypocrite, that detestable traitor, that prodigy of nature, that opprobrium of mankind, that landscape of iniquity, that sink of sin, and that compendium of baseness, who now calls himself our Protector."[14] Here is Vavasor Powell, a Welsh evangelist. He is best remembered for a pamphlet published from prison called *A Bird in a Cage Chirping Four Distinct Notes to Its Consorts Abroad*. This is what he is chirping in 1653: "Lord have our Army men all apostasized from their principles? What is become of all their declarations, protestations, and professions! Are they choked with lands, parks, and manors? . . . Let us go home and pray, and say, 'Lord wilt thou have Oliver Cromwell or Christ to reign over us?' "[15]

We could go on indefinitely, until we have seen how the suspicion of betrayal has eaten into saints who have fought and labored by his side for ten or fifteen years.

His own reaction varied. Sometimes he was angry. Especially in public speeches. We can see the tide of passion creating havoc with the syntax until he hits on a few short sentences that rap out his meaning: "I tell you I never sought this power! . . . I would have been glad to have lived under my woodside, to have kept a flock of sheep—rather than undertook such a Government as this is. . . . I am *called* to it. . . . If I am wrong, God will let me fall. . . . Let God be judge between you and me!"[16] Whereupon the saints he is addressing cry an angry "Amen," and the ordeal by battle, or maneuver, is duly joined.

But more often he is calm. With the persevering quiet that is more impressive than his anger. The kind of calm he shows on the eve of the Battle of Dunbar, when it seems as though only a miracle can prevent him from being defeated.[17] Or the simple resolution of this family letter to his son-in-law:

The Bankrupt Crusade

DEAR CHARLES,

Although I do not so often as is desired by me acquaint you how it is with me, yet I doubt not of your prayers in my behalf, that, in all things, I may walk as becometh the Gospel. Truly I never more needed all helps from my Christian friends than now! Fain would I have my service accepted of the saints (if the Lord will), but it is not so. Being of different judgments, and of each sort most seeking to propagate their own, that spirit of kindness that is [in me] to them all, is hardly accepted of any. I hope I can say it, my life has been a willing sacrifice. . . . Yet it much falls out as when the two Hebrews were rebuked: you know upon whom they turned their displeasure.[18]

But the Lord is wise, and will, I trust, make manifest that I am no enemy. Oh, how easy is mercy to be abused: Persuade friends with you to be very sober. If the day of the Lord be so near (as some say), how should our moderation appear. If every one (instead of contending) would justify his form "of judgment" by love and meekness, Wisdom would be justified of her children. But alas, I am, in my temptation, ready to say, Oh, would I had wings like a dove, then would I, etc.: but this, I fear, is my haste. I bless the Lord I have somewhat keeps me alive, some sparks of the light of His countenance, and some sincerity above man's judgment. Excuse me thus unbowelling myself to you: . . . My love to thy dear Wife, whom indeed I entirely love . . . and my blessings (if it be worth anything) upon thy little babe.[19]

Perhaps he kept that kind of faith. But he certainly lost some of the radiant insight into the Divine which Thomas Carlyle always found in him. In the five years which elapse between the Barebone's Parliament of 1653 and his death in 1658 he is substituting the guidance of mundane common sense for the promptings of the illuminated spirit. The Barebone's Parliament was an assembly of nominated saints which had nothing in common with a Parliament except the name, and his speech to it burns with an enthusiasm which is almost millenarian. But a few months later he procured its dissolution with the sorrowful comment that, where he once had knaves to deal with, he now had fools. He was spared one source of disillusionment. Unlike every other Puritan leader, he never felt the full weight of failure; never had to say, like the Scots after they had been mauled in the Battle of Dunbar, "God has hidden his face from the sons of Jacob,"[20] or, like Fleetwood, after the whole crusade is over, "God has spit in our faces." To the man who had taught himself to regard the verdict of success as the proof of Divine favor, this meant much. But there was certainly some surrender of the vision, as each attempt at settlement failed, as the forms of government drifted slowly back to monarchy, as foreign policy taught its hard lessons to the crusader, and as his godly Army began to turn insensibly into a professional force, held together more by discipline and pay than by the hope of salvation. To all skeptical eyes he presented the spectacle of the completely successful adventurer: the self-made ruler who had seized power and was holding it with a superb mastery of practical politics. What he thought of himself it would be hard to say. He had spoken as though he was a Moses who would lead his people to the Promised Land; then as a Moses who would never see the Promised Land; and sometimes as though he was just like other rulers who had received no promises at all. "Is it possible to fall from grace?" he is said to have asked the preachers as he lay dying, "for I know that I was once in grace." Of course they reassured him, not only about his salvation, but about his return to health. It seemed unthinkable that God should let such a worthy instrument die. But the great man was tired as well as puzzled. When they pressed him to drink something and to try to sleep, he replied: "It is not my design to drink or to sleep; my design is to make what haste I can to be gone."[21] The man who had never lost a battle was at last ordering a retreat.

The removal of this towering figure exposed all the frustrations of the crusade. While never ceasing to talk its language and to believe in what he said, he had actually been leading it back to sobriety. If he had lived, he would have made himself king and tried to consolidate the House of Cromwell. For that to have succeeded, many things would have been necessary, but among them one in particular: more and more compromises, until the English people acquired enough confidence in the House of Cromwell to renounce the House of Stuart. Dying when he did, what he left behind, besides all the secular elements with a vested interest in the Revolution, was something which called itself a crusade but was in fact a cluster of chieftains and factions which was absolutely incapable of organizing a stable government.

I do not propose here to trace the contortions of this doomed revolution. They last for some eighteen months —between September, 1658, and March, 1660. Power remains where it has been since the execution of the king—in the Army. But the Army, which has already lost its soul—the soldiers being only interested in pay, and the generals deeply committed to the protection of their estates and their careers—now loses its political senses. Trapped in the problem which Cromwell could not solve, egged on by doctrinaires of one description or another, it makes and breaks governments in a way that only plunges the country deeper into chaos. There is nothing quite like it as a study of futility. Old war cries are sounded, old gestures repeated; combinations tried which have failed before, and others dreamed up which only the most infatuated could expect to succeed.

It is characteristic of these situations to find hope still flaring in the midst of despair. Milton thinks the situation can be saved if the Army will only erect a perpetual senate of saints.[22] Baxter publishes a proposal called *A Holy Commonwealth*, in which all the resources of learning and piety are used to suggest that every offense which deserved death in the Old Testament—blasphemy, idolatry, adultery, disobedience to the priest, Sabbath-breaking—ought to be punished by disfranchisement in modern England. He asks, "Are the Irish fit to govern or choose Governours? If not; and if experience forceth us to exclude the main body of the Natives there, we have reason to exclude such here as forfeit their Liberties. We do them neither wrong nor hurt, but preserve ourselves from ruine and them from greater guilt. *To govern us, does them no good.*"[23] There, indeed, speaks the elect!

What sustained the saints was their conviction that God had been with them. If the past twenty years had not meant that, what had it meant? They had been *called* and, if only they could prove worthy, they were bound to succeed. The remedy for failure lay in repentance. That had always succeeded. Why should it not succeed now? But of course they are doomed; and no prayers, no humiliations, no appeals for universal holiness, no amount of constitution-making by juntos of military saints or desperate maneuvers by cliques of parliamentary saints can save them. After conjuring all sorts of human miracles out of their own exertions in the past twenty years, they have at last put themselves into a position where they really need a Divine one. And it does not come.

What comes is a Stuart Restoration. The last gambles of the military saints are neutralized by a massive campaign of passive and active resistance and by the decision of a cold professional soldier, General Monk, at the head of one compact segment of the Cromwellian Army, to align himself with the national demand for a free Parliament which would invite the Stuarts back again. Royalists, Presbyterians, and the mass of outraged Englishmen combined to make that possible. John Milton chose this moment to print a tract entitled *The Ready and Easy Way To Establish a Free Commonwealth*. But a cheering multitude were soon streaming down the road to Dover to greet a returning exile, Charles II, who remarked, with his usual wit, when he heard the cheers, that it must have been his own fault that he had been away so long. He then paid his compliments to the rule of the saints by kissing the Bible and describing it as the book he loved best in the world.

How did the saints accept their defeat? Some recanted to save their necks. Some recanted, found their courage again, and died in prison. Some went to the scaffold with the spirit of heroes and the faith that the miracle which had not come would follow their deaths. Some went into exile. They are last seen on the frontiers of Massachusetts defending a village against an Indian attack or brooding in Switzerland over the treacheries that wrecked so glorious a cause. One writes *Paradise Lost.* Another writes the *Pilgrim's Progress* in a Bedford jail. A third makes a last bid for the millennium by starting an insurrection in the streets of London.

As for the main body, whether the Center and Left, or the Presbyterians who helped to produce the Restoration only to find themselves persecuted by their Anglican allies in the subsequent settlement, they renounce any hopes of making England a holy community. Their claim on the state, which they had tried to force into a Puritan mold for the past century, is now a claim for toleration. Baxter, who wrote the *Holy Commonwealth* in 1659, has this to say a few years later:

> I am farther than ever I was from expecting great matters of unity, splendour, or prosperity to the Church on earth, or that saints should dream of a kingdom of this world, or flatter themselves with the hopes of a golden age, or reigning over the ungodly. . . . On the contrary, I am more apprehensive that suffering must be the church's ordinary lot, and Christians indeed must be self-denying cross-bearers, even where there are none but formal, nominal Christians to be the cross-makers; and though ordinarily God would have vicissitudes of summer and winter, day and night, that the church may grow extensively in the summer of prosperity and intensively in the winter of adversity, yet usually their night is longer than their day, and that day itself hath its storms and tempests.[24]

The winter of adversity never lifted for Richard Baxter. When "cross-making" was abandoned by the English government in 1689, for a regime of religious toleration, it was in a world more "formal and nominal," in its attachment to Christianity, than any Puritan had ever known.

The Puritan Tradition

How does one assess the influence of some profound experience on the subsequent history of a people? The effort of these Puritan saints to seize and dominate the life of English-speaking people in the seventeenth century was obviously such an experience, and everyone who inspects the national consciousness of Englishmen and Americans today finds Puritanism a part of its makeup, whether the inspection is made by ourselves or by strangers who look at us with the incredulity—sometimes kindly, sometimes irritated—of visitors from another world.[1] But what is this Puritanism which has a continuing history? Obviously, it is not the Puritanism which I have been discussing in this book. That is a historical movement with a beginning and an end. It does not repeat itself. Nor is the Puritanism with a continuing history the sum total of the connections which can be traced to Puritanism. Unitarianism can be traced to Puritanism and Transcendentalism to Unitarianism, but is Emerson to be regarded as part of the Puritan tradition? I should say "Yes" only if it could be shown that Emerson was attempting to solve his problems as he believed that Puritans tried to solve theirs or if his solutions bore some direct resemblance to Puritan solutions. Let me foreshorten this type of question and make it more extreme. There were Puritans in the seventeenth century who telescoped into their own lives a history which might take fifty years to work itself out in a dissenting congregation; that is to say, they began as dogmatic Puritans with an intense conviction of their election and ended as lukewarm deists with a few Puritan inhibitions. Is such a man to be considered a Puritan after he has worked his passage from the ages of faith into the ages of reason? I should say not, if the term is to have any meaning at all. Similarly, I should say that the continuing history of Puritanism, if it is to have any useful meaning, must be the continuing history of attempts to solve problems in a Puritan spirit.

To limit it to this is still to leave it sufficiently ambiguous, for it is in the nature of such attempts that they represent selections and adaptations of the original experience. Let me give an example. When the statue of Oliver Cromwell, with his Bible and his sword, which stands in the shadow of the House of Commons, was unveiled toward the close of the last century, the address was given by the Earl of Rosebery. It was a symbolic occasion: the final touch in the adoption of Cromwell as a national hero. After vindicating his essential honesty from all the old charges of ambition and hypocrisy and explaining that the secret of his strength lay in the fact that he was a practical mystic, Rosebery continues: "We could find employment for a few Cromwells now. . . . The Cromwell of the nineteenth or the twentieth centuries would not naturally be the Cromwell of the seventeenth. . . . He would not decapitate; he would not rise in revolution or speak the Puritan language. But he would retain his essential qualities as general, as ruler, as statesman. He would be strenuous. He would be sincere. He would not compromise with principles. His faith would be in God and in freedom, and in the influence of Great Britain as promoting both. . . . I know there are some individuals to whom this theory is cant. . . . I know it and I am sorry for them. I believe that the vast majority of our people are inspired by a nobler creed; that their Imperialism, as it is called, is not the lust of dominion or the pride of power, but rather the ideal of Oliver."[2]

Victorian England is making its own appropriation of the Puritan tradition. Puritan itself, it derives strength and purpose from its Puritan past, but it takes what it can use and transforms it in the taking.

Thomas Carlyle might serve as another example. He came from a Calvinist home where he learned the same lessons as the Puritans from the same sacred Book. Like them, he encountered the unbelief and false belief of his generation. He passed through an experience of conversion and discovered his mission in a prophetic ministry. His overpowering sense of divinity, of moral law, of human sin, and of the duty of man to save himself through strenuous self-denial is the same as theirs. He writes their history with an insight into the Puritan soul which few people have ever equaled and trumpets to the modern world that only in deep-hearted believing spirits like Oliver Cromwell will they find the true saviors of society. However, he belongs to no church; he cannot believe that Scripture is literally true; he buries, in what he calls a wise silence, all sorts of questions to which the Puritans had dogmatic answers; and he has enlarged the fraternity of believers to include a pantheon of pagans which would have stupefied his Calvinist ancestors.

But, when all this has been said, the fact remains that the gulf between them is theological rather than moral. If the life of man begins in darkness and ends in darkness, the lesson is to cling all the more passionately to the feeling that there is some kind of order behind the mystery and that this order reveals itself most clearly in the moral sense. And the moral sense to which Carlyle appeals is indestructibly Puritan.

Here, then, is another appropriation of the Puritan tradition. Occasionally the appropriator has some idea of what Puritanism originally stood for and of the kind of selection he is making. No one needed to tell either Rosebery or Carlyle that the Puritan's zeal for freedom was always being overcome by his passion for righteousness and that, if that meant knocking Irish priests over the head or governing Englishmen through major generals, he could do it with a good conscience. Rosebery rejected that side of the Puritan; Carlyle kept it. He was fond of saying that Oliver Cromwell was the best friend poor Ireland ever had.[3] But the appropriator is not usually as familiar with the original Puritans as either Rosebery or Carlyle, and he endows them with all sorts of qualities that they never possessed. However, to say this is only to say that we are dealing with a creative tradition: something which performs its operational function of directing responses to changing situations and which is entitled to bear the original name so long as it shows some correspondence with the original spirit.

The Puritan Tradition

If one is looking for the broadest definition of the original Puritanism, it obviously falls into the category of religious revivals. This has been a recurring rhythm in the history of Christian culture, and a more general view than I am taking in these essays would relate Puritanism to earlier revivals. However, if one is to ignore this previous history, and to start with Puritanism, one finds that it has certain drive and that it goes through the typical history of self-discovery, enthusiasm, organization, and decay. It derives its drive from its view of the human predicament. When the Puritan surveys the world within the terms laid down by Christian tradition, he is struck by the profundity of human sin, by the necessity for a work of grace in his own soul to redeem him from the lot of fallen humanity, and by the demand for a disciplined warfare against sin which God makes on those he has saved. His pilgrimage is therefore a search for regeneration, which is usually achieved through an experience of conversion, and for the development of the type of character which is appropriate to the regenerate—a character marked by an intense sense of personal responsibility to God and his moral law, which expresses itself in a strenuous life of self-examination and self-denial. So much for the drive. As for the typical history, it takes rather more than a century to work itself out. The origins of English Puritanism are to be found among the Protestant Reformers of the mid-sixteenth century; it takes shape in the reign of Elizabeth; produces thrust after thrust of energy in the seventeenth century, until the final thrust throws up the Quakers; and then ebbs away.

This revival is clearly followed by another, working within the same tradition, having a similar drive, and much the same scope in time. The low-water mark between the two is obviously in the first half of the eighteenth century. If I may take an arbitrary symbol for the state of religious life in England—something which is suggestive without pretending to be representative—I would use a casual pleasantry from one of the witty letter-writers of the period, the Lady Mary Wortley Montagu. "I was told," she said, "by a very good author, who is deep in the secret, that at this very minute there is a bill cooking up at a hunting-seat in Norfolk, to have *not* taken out of the commandments and clapped into the creed, the ensuing session of Parliament . . . honour, virtue, reputation, etc., which we used to hear of in our nursery, is as much laid aside and forgotten as crumpled ribbons."[4] I need hardly say that Massachusetts never fell as low as that. But if, in this period, New England has an established Puritan church, with the flag of the Covenant pinned firmly to the masthead of the community, the Puritanism which exists there has been diluted and confused by the same forces which have had a freer field in the country where Puritanism failed to capture the community.

Now turn from the Lady Mary, who wrote her letter in 1723, to John Wesley's *Journal* of May 24, 1738. "I went," he writes, "very unwillingly to a society in Aldersgate Street, where one was reading Luther's Preface to the Epistle to the Romans. About a quarter before nine, while he was describing the change which God works in the heart through faith in

Christ, I felt my heart strangely warmed. I felt I did trust in Christ, Christ alone, for my salvation. And an assurance was given me that he had taken away *my* sins, even *mine*, and saved *me* from the law of sin and death."[5] Three days before, his brother Charles Wesley had also been converted, in his case through Luther's Commentary on the Epistle to the Galatians, which had been the instrument of John Bunyan's conversion. Add to this experience of conversion this glimpse of the life of the converted, which is taken from Wesley's rules for the communion of saints and which might be described as the Puritan's version of the priesthood of all believers:

"The design of our meeting is, to obey that command of God, 'Confess your faults one to another, and pray for one another that ye may be healed.' . . . Do you desire to be told of all your faults and that plain and home? Consider! Do you desire we should tell you whatsoever we think, whatsoever we fear, whatsoever we hear, concerning you? Do you desire that, in doing this, we should come as close as possible, that we should cut to the quick, and search your heart to the bottom? . . . You are supposed to have the faith that overcometh the world."[6]

This has a familiar ring. Equally familiar are the series of sermons which Jonathan Edwards had delivered in Massachusetts a few years before and the Great Awakening which followed them. On both sides of the Atlantic the same symptoms have appeared; they quickly reinforce each other, and they form the beginning of an evangelical movement which continues to pulse through the English-speaking people until it reaches a climax of influence in the second half of the nineteenth century, and then once again ebbs away. In America it is the chief means through which the Protestant churches undertake the enormous task of Christianizing a continent. In Britain there is the same problem of impressing religion and morality on an expanding population both at home and overseas.

I have already touched on some of the contrasts between this second revival and the first. Let me make some of them more explicit.

One contrast lies in the relationship between the Puritan and the intellect of his age. Though I have said in a previous chapter that I think the picture of the Puritan as an intellectual has been overdrawn, to the extent that Puritanism was always more an affair of the heart than of the head, the fact remains that the earlier Puritan did not have to maintain his faith in spite of or against the evidences of philosophy or science. Many Puritans, in my definition, which includes the anti-intellectuals as well as the intellectuals, were neither interested in these evidences nor capable of judging them, but those who were could feel that the truths of Scripture were in harmony with all learning and experience. There was much in the philosophic tradition to support the Puritan. There was little in historical science to shake his faith in Scripture or his conception of human history as the field in which God gathers his elect. There was nothing in the older physical science to cause him great concern: no mechanistic theory of the universe, no displacement of this planet from its central place, no doctrine of evolution. His use of the prophetic books of the Bible to interpret human history, his doctrine of special providences in which God was constantly setting aside the ordinary operations of nature to achieve his purposes, seemed eminently reasonable to him. The result was that among the Puritan scholastics—the last representatives of the medieval ambition to synthesize all experience—it was possible to achieve a fusion of intellect and emotion that was less and less possible for their descendants. Increasingly, it becomes necessary to bury difficult questions in a wise silence or to compromise with them in a way which robs the Puritan impulse of some of its otherworldliness or to shunt them aside. On the whole, evangelism has chosen either to bury or to shunt. Although it has been able to impart its ethical impulse to almost all classes of society, so that even the high aristocrat in Victorian England cultivates a sense of duty and the agnostic himself is a very earnest moralist, it has been less and less able to sound intellectually respectable. And in its extremer forms it becomes a religion of feeling without any intellectual structure at all.

The second contrast lies in the relationship between the Puritan and the religious organization of his society. When the first revival began, his society had a dogmatic religious commitment, and no such thing as toleration existed, apart from the concessions which politicians have always made to expediency. Working within this tradition, the first impulse of the Puritan was to turn his community into a rigorous theocracy. Government of the people, by and for the saints, might be described as his idea of good government. However, partly as a result of divisions among the saints, and of the genuine theory of religious liberty which some saints developed, and partly as the result of developments for which the saints can claim no credit, what emerged from that enterprise was not a theocracy but a regime of toleration. The second revival begins under that regime. In America it is turned into a regime of religious liberty, with the state separated from the church. The diversity of religions left no alternative so far as the federal government was concerned, and the rationalists combined with the evangelicals to get the state churches disestablished. In Britain, religious toleration is turned into a system where no religion is discriminated against, but an established church remains. All this means that the second revival is working within either a liberal or a democratic community. But its theocratic impulse dies hard. The converted soul is likely to cling to its conviction that it has a superior insight into God's design for the social order—a conviction which irritates the unconverted and which is not based on any experience. The belief of Roger Williams that the state should be left to the natural reason which God has bestowed on all his creatures, with the Christian only playing his part as one witness, would seem to be more appropriate. However, if political leaders, like Lincoln, are sometimes afflicted by preachers who insist that God demands the immediate abolition of slavery, these reformers are no longer in a position to use any force but argument.

So much for the obvious contrasts. As for the comparisons, there is the conversion experience, which I have chosen as the central feature of the original Puritanism. There is the fission process, the endless splintering, the Babel of heresies, or the flowering of the sects, whichever you prefer to call it—a process which demonstrates once again how fundamental the individualism of the Protestant Reformation has proved to be compared with its superficial collectivism. There is, furthermore, the same bewildering variety of consequences which the search for regeneration can have; the same variety as it had during the Puritan Revolution. Some activities no doubt tend to be shared: an educational mission, a philanthropic mission, a mission to preserve Sabbatarianism or to promote the adoption of Puritan morals, an evangelical impulse which prompts the converted to adopt causes of one description or another. But in this last category it is noticeable that the southern churches feel little disposition to adopt the antislavery cause and that the conversion experience is compatible with every kind of social outlook. John Wesley is a Tory, but the movement he starts will produce liberals, chartists, and socialists. English nonconformity, smarting under the legal privileges and social snobberies of parsons and squires, is either middle or lower class; but English evangelicalism will make as many converts within the privileged classes as outside. Jacksonian democrats like Orestes Brownson are in the tradition of seventeenth-century Levellers, and they are resisted by Puritans in the tradition of seventeenth-century Brahmins. Evangelicalism can mean an individualistic search for salvation or a social gospel. It can reinforce capitalism or produce experiments in communism. It can sustain the privileged or rally the underprivileged. The insights of the converted, as they survey the social scene, are simply not to be marshaled under any single formula.

The final similarity is, of course, in the character. I have said enough in this book about the heroic virtues. The defects have often been made the subject of jibes, and I shall try to restrain myself.

The Puritan has a very limited sense of humor, as one can see from a glance at his portrait. I am thinking not of Grant Wood's "American Gothic" but of seventeenth-century portraits. The corners of the mouths in the divines, at least, are almost invariably pulled down. Emerson has a good phrase for his ancestors. He calls them "the great grim earnest men who solemnized the heyday of their strength by planting New England." I will only add that life seldom struck them as funny. I know that the historian of New England can produce one humorist in Nathaniel Ward; but I have not been so fortunate with the English Puritans. The nearest I came to it was in a Puritan diary, where the author admits he cannot repress his desire to tell a good story, but he tries to keep the account straight by capping every joke with what he calls "a savoury morsel" of divinity. Cromwell's characteristic humor is a sort of horseplay; this is the Cromwell who throws cushions at his officers, who is said to have spattered an officer's face with ink while they were signing the king's death warrant, or who gets a good laugh watching a soldier tip a pail of milk over another soldier's head. Perhaps it is a relief from tension with a touch of hysteria about it; or perhaps it is just the bucolic antics of a plain russet-coated captain. Later in the history of Puritanism a certain humor develops, but it is naturally rather wry—or it has to be indulged when the great Taskmaster is not looking. Of course I do not want to imply that the Puritan, while he is being a Puritan, cannot make a good remark. I have always liked the reply of the revivalist preacher who had not much grammar and was one day ridiculed for it. "That's all right, brother; what little I have I use for the Lord. What do you do with yours?"[7] But you see he is keeping his eye on the main business. Of all the gifts of humor, the only one which blends naturally with the Puritan's purpose is satire: the sort of satire which Carlyle used to such effect in producing conversions.

The other defects of the Puritan character all spring from the fact that he has stripped himself of nonessentials for the struggle and finds it grim. He makes very little contribution to literature outside the didactic sphere. He is likely to regard the arts as the trimmings of life. And he can degenerate into a kill-joy. Macaulay's jibe about the reason why the Puritans suppressed bear-baiting has a grain of symbolic truth in it. They suppressed it, not because it gave pain to the bear, but because it gave pleasure to the spectators.

In conclusion, let us return to the Puritan's impact on politics. Among his virtues I would list:

1. *His contribution to our system of limited government.*—The original Puritans had a genuine basis for their distrust of arbitrary power in addition to their experience of arbitrary government. They thought that man was too sinful to be trusted with too much power. They were likely to make an exception of the saint, but, once saints were prevented from ruling, they have kept their conviction that nobody else

should be trusted. The Puritan tradition, with its everlasting insistence that only God is worthy of worship, is one insurance among Anglo-Saxon people that the state has no claim to worship. Fortunately, there are many other securities, but no one will undervalue the stubbornness of this one. They have defended, in season and out of season, the right to preach, to criticize, and to judge. A shrewd observer of the English scene after the Puritan Revolution was struck by the difference it had made to the power of authority to procure respect for its pronouncements: "He [the author] thinketh that the Liberty of the late times gave men so much Light, and diffused its so universally amongst the people, that they are not now to be dealt with, as they might have been in Ages of less enquiry; and therefore tho in some well chosen and dearly beloved Auditories, good resolute Nonsense back'd with Authority may prevail, yet generally Men are become so good Judges of what they hear, that the Clergy ought to be very wary how they go about to impose upon their Understandings, which are grown less humble than they were in former times, when the Men in black had made Learning such a sin in the Laity, that for fear of offending, they made a Conscience of being able to read; but now the World is grown sawcy, and expecteth Reasons, and good ones too, before they give up their own Opinions to other Mens Dictates, tho never so Magisterially deliver'd to them."[8]

2. *His contribution to self-government—to the development of initiative and self-reliance in the body of the community.*—The Puritan pilgrimage has been a perpetual pilgrimage in self-help. The significance of the dissent-

ing chapel as a training ground for working-class leadership in English history has often been emphasized, and much the same services have been performed by the free church tradition in America. Nor should we forget, in the nineteenth century as in the seventeenth, the direct transfer from church affairs to political affairs of certain techniques of action. The political meeting of the nineteenth century owes an obvious, if not wholly healthy, debt to the camp meeting of the revivalist preacher.

3. *His contribution to education.*—The most anti-intellectual Puritan has been obliged to master at least one book—and that a great one. The most intellectual Puritans, in their desire to promote saving knowledge, have thrown up academy after academy, college after college, until their influence has been writ large over the history of education in England and America.

4. *His contribution to morality.*—The Puritan code has its repellent features, but it is no bad thing to have habits of honesty, sobriety, responsibility, and hard work impressed on a community. It seems probable that the acquisitive energy of the nineteenth century would have created far more havoc than it did without the restraining influence of this evangelical spirit.

Finally, there is the contribution which Puritanism, within the religious tradition of Anglo-Saxon peoples, has made to "the class peace." Almost the worst thing that can happen to the politics of a modern society is to have them polarized around social classes. Any force which works across these divisions, and either conceals or cements them, has a permanent claim on our gratitude.

Puritanism in Old and New England

As the limitations of Puritanism have been sufficiently stressed in these essays, I shall quote only one passage which seems to sum them up. I might have chosen for censure the *cri de cœur* of the nonconformist conscience in nineteenth-century English politics as it appears in the protest of the famous preacher Hugh Price Hughes: "What is morally wrong can never be politically right." Instead, I shall take a passage from an American sermon called "Puritan Principles and the Modern World," which was delivered in 1897:

"Puritanism stands for reality; for character; for clean living as a condition of public service; for recognition of responsibility to God; for the supremacy of the spirit. When Oliver Cromwell entered Parliament in 1653, and said, pointing to one member, 'There sits a taker of bribes'; to another, 'There sits a man whose religion is a farce'; to another, using the hardest name possible, which I soften, 'There sits a man whose personal conduct is impure and foul'; and then in the name of Almighty God broke up the Parliament, he was the impersonation of Puritanism; and for one, I wish he would rise from his grave and in the same spirit enter some of our halls of legislation, both state and national."[9]

That passage, with its conviction that righteousness ought to prevail, with its tendency to make the Puritan's own moral character a test of political fitness, and with its pressure to turn politics, which ought to be the art of reconciliation, into a moral crusade, reminds us of the darkest blot on his political record.

Notes

CHAPTER I

1. E.g., Perry Miller, *Orthodoxy in Massachusetts, 1630–1650* (Cambridge, Mass.: Harvard University Press, 1933), and W. K. Jordan, *The Development of Religious Toleration in England* (3 vols.; London, G. Allen & Unwin, 1932–38).

2. E.g., A. S. P. Woodhouse, *Puritanism and Liberty* (London: J. M. Dent & Sons, 1938). It was Professor Woodhouse who provided the classic analysis of Puritanism in terms of its Right, Center, and Left factions.

3. *Ibid.*, p. xxxvii: "It is unnecessary to posit a unity in all Puritan thought; it is sufficient to recognise a continuity." Though excluding the Quakers from his study, Professor Woodhouse was well aware of the continuity of spiritual experience linking Dell, Collier, Erbury, Lilburne, and Winstanley with George Fox (*ibid.*, p. xxxviii).

4. For Cromwell's use of the phrase see the remark on the qualifications for the ministry in his state church: "Though a man be of any of those three judgments [i.e., Presbyterian, Independent, Baptist], if he have the root of the matter in him he may be admitted" (C. H. Firth, *Oliver Cromwell* [London: Putnam, 1947], p. 359).

5. Thomas Goodwin, *Works* (London, 1704), pp. v–xix.

6. *The Letters and Speeches of Oliver Cromwell with Elucidations by Thomas Carlyle*, ed. S. C. Lomas (London: Methuen & Co., 1904), I, 89–90.

7. Puritans acknowledged the possibility that the saint might have grown into his condition without any recollection of a violent rebirth (see A. S. P. Woodhouse, "Notes on Milton's Early Development," *University of Toronto Quarterly*, XIII [1943–44], 73–74). But it was sufficiently unusual for it to be a matter of anxiety to some of the godly that they could not date their conversion.

8. This was one of Cromwell's favorite descriptions (see Titus 2:14: "Who gave himself for us, that he might redeem us from all iniquity, and purify unto himself a peculiar people, zealous of good

works"; and I Pet. 2:9: "But ye are a chosen generation, a royal priesthood, an holy nation, a peculiar people; that ye should shew forth the praises of him who hath called you out of darkness into his marvellous light").

The following statement by Richard Sibbes, a famous prewar preacher, is sufficiently succinct to deserve quotation: "1. As the ground of all the rest, wee apprehend God to be a God of some peculiar persons, as *favourites* above others. 2. From hence is stirred up in the soule a restlesse desire, that God would discover himselfe so to it, as hee doth to those that are *his*, that hee would *visit our soules* with the salvation *of his chosen*. 3. Hence followes a putting of the soule upon God, an adventuring it selfe on his mercy. 4. Upon this, God when he seeth fit, discovers by his spirit that hee is *Ours*. 5. Whence followeth a dependance on him as ours, for all things that may carry us on in the way to heaven" (*The Soules Conflict with Itselfe, and Victory over Itselfe by Faith: A Treatise of the Inward Disquietments of Distressed Spirits, with Comfortable Remedies To Establish Them* [3d ed.; London, 1636], pp. 550–51).

9. "He had either extinguished, or by habit had learned to subdue, the whole host of vain hopes, fears, and passions, which infest the soul. He first acquired the government of himself, and over himself acquired the most signal victories; so that on the first day he took the field against the external enemy, he was a veteran in arms" (John Milton, "The Second Defence of the People of England," *The Prose Works of John Milton*, ed. J. A. St. John [London: G. Bell & Sons, 1910], I, 286).

10. L. J. Trinterud, "Origins of Puritanism," *Church History*, XX (1951), 37–57.

11. William Perkins, *Works* (Cambridge, 1600), p. 1027 ("The Foundation of Christian Religion").

12. This was the characteristic dogma of the interwar historiography. So much so that the Puritan revolution—to the bewilderment of aging scholars in cloisters and clubs—was being fast turned into a bourgeois revolution. For crude statements of the dogma see Christopher Hill, *The English Revolution, 1640* (London: Lawrence & Wishart, 1940), and *The Good Old Cause* (London: Lawrence & Wishart, 1949); for a subtly ambiguous one see R. H. Tawney, *Religion and the Rise of Capitalism* (London: J. Murray, 1926).

13. Richard Baxter, *Reliquiae Baxterianae*, ed. M. Sylvester (London, 1696), p. 89: "And it was a great Advantage to me, that my

Neighbours were of such a Trade as allowed them time enough to read or talk of holy Things. For the Town liveth upon the Weaving of *Kidderminster* Stuffs; and as they stand in their Loom they can set a Book before them, or edifie one another: whereas Plowmen, and many others, are so wearied or continually employed, either in the Labours or the Cares of their Callings, that it is a great Impediment to their Salvation."

14. Edward, Earl of Clarendon, *Life* (2 vols.; Oxford, 1857), I, 47.
15. R. P. Stearns, *Congregationalism in the Dutch Netherlands* (Chicago: American Society of Church History, 1940).
16. "John Stubbs," *Dictionary of National Biography*.
17. Richard Baxter, *A Holy Commonwealth* (London, 1659), p. 457.
18. Thomas Hobbes, *The Elements of Law*, ed. Ferdinand Tönnies (Cambridge, 1928), pp. 113–14, 135–36.
19. Lord Macaulay, *Critical, Historical and Miscellaneous Essays* (New York: A. C. Armstrong & Son, 1860), p. 255 ("Milton").
20. E.g., Richard Baxter, *A Holy Commonwealth*, pp. 457 ff.; *Memoirs of the Life of Colonel Hutchinson*, ed. C. H. Firth (London: George Routledge & Sons, 1906), pp. 78–79.
21. Woodhouse, *Puritanism and Liberty*, p. xxxvii: "Puritanism means a determined and varied effort to erect the holy community and to meet, with different degrees of compromise and adjustment, the problem of its conflict with the world."

CHAPTER II

1. John Cotton, *Christ the Fountaine of Life: or, Sundry Choyce Sermons on Part of the Fifth Chapter of the First Epistle of St. John* (London, 1651), p. 148.
2. E.g., Perry Miller, *Orthodoxy in Massachusetts, 1630–1650* (Cambridge, Mass.: Harvard University Press, 1933); *The New England Mind: The Seventeenth Century* (New York: Macmillan Co., 1939); and *The New England Mind: From Colony to Province* (Cambridge, Mass.; Harvard University Press, 1953).
3. "It is impossible to conceive of a disillusioned Puritan; no matter what misfortune befell him, no matter how often or how tragically his fellowmen failed him, he would have been prepared for the worst, and would have expected no better" (Perry Miller and T. H. Johnson, *The Puritans* [New York: American Book Co., 1938], p. 60).

4. *The Letters and Speeches of Oliver Cromwell with Elucidations by Thomas Carlyle*, ed. S. C. Lomas (London: Methuen & Co., 1904), II, 299.

5. This remark was the reaction of Charles Fleetwood, commander-in-chief, to the discovery that the last gamble of the military saints, in the autumn of 1659, had failed (quoted by M. Guizot, *History of Richard Cromwell and the Restoration of Charles II* [London, 1856], II, 64).

6. The phrase is John Cotton's (quoted by Miller and Johnson, *op. cit.*, p. 61).

7. Winthrop Papers, II (Boston: Massachusetts Historical Society, 1931), 294. The spelling in the quotation has been modernized.

8. *Ibid.*, p. 293.

9. Edward Johnson, *Wonder-working Providence of Sions Saviour in New England* (Andover, Mass.: Warren F. Draper, 1867), pp. 95–96.

10. Professor Morison's determination to make humanists out of his Puritan ancestors appears in *Harvard College in the Seventeenth Century* (Cambridge, Mass.: Harvard University Press, 1936), p. 165; *Three Centuries of Harvard, 1636–1936* (Cambridge, Mass.: Harvard University Press, 1936), pp. 22–25; and *Puritan Pronaos* (New York: New York University Press, 1936), pp. 29–30, 39, 45, 52–53. The success of his efforts may be judged from Professor Miller's compliment: "Thanks to the labors of Professor Morison, we may now rest assured that the Puritans of New England were the disciples of Erasmus and Colet" (Miller and Johnson, *op. cit.*, p. 21). However, there have been skeptical voices (see W. S. Hudson, "The Morison Myth concerning the Founding of Harvard College," *Church History*, VIII [1939], 148–59). The problem is one of emphasis, but the end of all education in early New England is best stated simply as in E. S. Morgan's chapter on "The Education of a Saint," in *The Puritan Family* (Boston: Trustees of the Public Library, 1944), p. 47: "The main business of education was to prepare children for conversion."

11. See Miller, *Orthodoxy in Massachusetts*.

12. The correspondence between John Cotton and Lord Say and Seal, who was contemplating emigration in 1636, reflects the latter's anxiety on this point (Thomas Hutchinson, *History of Massachusetts Bay* [1764], I, Appendix III, 496–501).

13. *Bradford's History of Plymouth Plantation, 1606–1646*, ed. William T. Davis (New York: Charles Scribner's Sons, 1908), pp. 54–55.

14. *Ibid.*, p. 55.

15. Perry Miller, "The Half-Way Covenant," *New England Quarterly*, VI (1933), 703.

16. Samuel Danforth, *A Briefe Recognition of New Englands Errand into the Wilderness* (Cambridge, Mass., 1671), pp. 12–13.

17. *Diary of Samuel Sewall* ("Collections of the Massachusetts Historical Society: Fifth Series," Vol. V [Boston, 1878]), I, 444.

CHAPTER III

1. Voltaire, *Lettres philosophiques*, ed. G. Lanson (Paris: Société Nouvelle de Librairie et d'Édition, 1909), I, 74.

2. Roger Williams, *Experiments of Spiritual Life and Health*, ed. W. S. Hudson (Philadelphia: Westminster Press, 1951).

3. Letter to Major Mason, June 22, 1670, *Publications of the Narragansett Club* (Providence, R.I., 1866–74), VI, 347.

4. This quotation is a paraphrase of the position adopted by Ireton in the Whitehall Debates of 1648. For his own words see A. S. P. Woodhouse, *Puritanism and Liberty* (London: J. M. Dent & Sons, 1938), pp. 146, 150, 154–56, 162, 166–68.

5. For an enthusiastic explanation of Williams' use of typology see Perry Miller's excellent guide to his writings, *Roger Williams: His Contribution to the American Tradition* (New York: Bobbs-Merrill Co., 1953).

6. Roger Williams, "The Bloody Tenent of Persecution," *Publications of the Narragansett Club*, Vol. III, chap. cxxxvii.

7. For Samuel Gorton see K. W. Porter, "Samuel Gorton, New England Firebrand," *New England Quarterly*, VII (1934), 405–44.

8. [Clement Walker,] *Anarchia Anglicana: Or the History of Independency* (London, 1649), Part II, pp. 152–53.

9. Porter, *op. cit.*, p. 417.

10. This thesis is reflected in V. L. Parrington, *Main Currents in American Thought* (New York: Harcourt, Brace & Co., 1927), I, 64; J. E. Ernst, *The Political Thought of Roger Williams* (Seattle: University of Washington Press, 1929), p. 25; and S. H. Brockunier, *The Irrepressible Democrat: Roger Williams* (New York: Ronald Press, 1940).

11. Brockunier, *op. cit.*, pp. 166, 280. In these two cases, a criticism of the proprietorship at Taunton (p. 166) and an appeal to the town of Providence (p. 280) are used to support the thesis. In the first, Williams is protesting against clerical exploitation; in the

second, he is pleading for a pittance for religious refugees. No vision of an "equalitarian" democracy is involved in either of them.

12. *Publications of the Narragansett Club*, VI, 319.

13. George Sikes, *Life and Death of Sir Henry Vane, or a Short Narrative of the Main Passages of His Earthly Pilgrimage* (1662), p. 3.

14. Porter, *op. cit.*, p. 443.

CHAPTER IV

1. For Harrington's explanation of the breakdown of the monarchy see *The Commonwealth of Oceana*, ed. John Toland (London, 1771), pp. 63–65. For the most succinct statement of his theories see "A System of Politics Delineated in Short and Easy Aphorisms," *ibid.*, p. 465.

2. David Hume, *History of England* (London, 1778), VI, 47–49; and *Essays and Treatises* (London, 1758), p. 21.

3. See R. H. Tawney, "The Rise of the Gentry," *Economic History Review*, Vol. XI, No. 1 (1941), and "Harrington's Interpretation of His Age," *Proceedings of the British Academy*, XXVII (1941), 199–223. Aspects of Professor Tawney's thesis have been vigorously criticized by H. R. Trevor-Roper, "The Gentry, 1540–1640," *Economic History Review*, Supplement No. 1 (April, 1953); but this interesting controversy should not disturb the obvious fact that the gentry were gaining in relative wealth and power, compared with the monarchy, the peerage, and the church.

4. See "A Declaration of the English Army Now in Scotland, 1 August, 1650," and "A Glimpse of Sion's Glory, 1641," in A. S. P. Woodhouse, *Puritanism and Liberty* (London: J. M. Dent & Sons, 1938), pp. 474–75, 233.

5. E.g., John Hutchinson, who, according to his wife, was immersed in the contemplation of God's absolute decrees, and his own election, when the excitements of 1641 forced him to look into the issues that were being debated at Westminster. He came to the conclusion that Parliament was justified "in point of civil right"; but, "thinking he had no warrantable call at that time to do anything more, contented himself with praying for peace" (*Memoirs of the Life of Colonel Hutchinson*, ed. C. H. Firth [London: George Routledge & Sons, 1906], pp. 78–79).

6. Richard Baxter, *A Holy Commonwealth* (London, 1659), p. 457.

7. For Cromwell's account of this decision see the famous remi-

niscence of a conversation with John Hampden in 1642: " 'Your troopers,' said I, 'are most of them old decayed serving-men, and tapsters, and such kind of fellows; and,' said I, 'their troopers are gentlemen's sons, younger sons and persons of quality. . . .' I did tell him: 'You must get men of a spirit . . . that is likely to go on as far as gentlemen will go. . . .' He did think that I talked a good notion, but an impracticable one. Truly I told him I could do somewhat in it. I did so . . . I raised such men as had the fear of God before them, and made some conscience of what they did; and from that day forward, I must say to you, they were never beaten" (speech to Parliament, April 13, 1657 [*The Letters and Speeches of Oliver Cromwell with Elucidations by Thomas Carlyle*, ed. S. C. Lomas (London: Methuen & Co., 1904), III, 65–66]).

8. *The Works of John Owen*, ed. W. H. Goold (Edinburgh: T. & T. Clark, 1862), VIII, 405.

9. For Ireton's view of the causes of the revolution, and of the relative importance of civil and religious issues, see his own statements (Woodhouse, *op. cit.*, pp. 72, 174, 458–59).

10. Richard Baxter, *Reliquiae Baxterianae*, ed. M. Sylvester (London, 1696), p. 53.

11. S. R. Gardiner, *History of the Commonwealth and Protectorate* (4 vols.; London: Longmans, Green & Co., 1903), I, 35.

12. The funeral of Robert Lockyer, April 27, 1649 (*ibid.*, pp. 46–47).

13. The acquittal of John Lilburne, August 20, 1653 (*ibid.*, II, 298).

14. "A Glimpse of Sion's Glory" (Woodhouse, *op. cit.*, pp. 233–34).

15. "Certain Queries Presented by Many Christian People" (1649) (*ibid.*, pp. 244–45).

CHAPTER V

1. S. R. Gardiner, *History of the Great Civil War* (4 vols.; London: Longmans, Green & Co., 1898), II, 59.

2. Edmund Burke, *Speeches and Letters on American Affairs* ("Everyman's Library" [London: J. M. Dent & Sons, 1942]), p. 93.

3. A. S. P. Woodhouse, *Puritanism and Liberty* (London: J. M. Dent & Sons, 1950), p. 415.

4. This argument was used by Cromwell. "They would have put into his hands all that we had engaged for, and all our security would have been a little bit of paper." The reference is to the New-

port negotiations between Parliament and the king which the Army broke off after its return from the field (C. H. Firth, *Oliver Cromwell* [London: Putnam, 1947], p. 212).

5. "The Lord at thy right hand shall strike through kings in the day of his wrath" (Ps. 110:5). Cromwell once took an hour to explain to Ludlow how the prophecies in this psalm were being accomplished (*Memoirs of Edmund Ludlow*, ed. C. H. Firth [Oxford, 1894], I, 246).

6. *The Letters and Speeches of Oliver Cromwell with Elucidations by Thomas Carlyle*, ed. S. C. Lomas (London: Methuen & Co., 1904), I, 305–10.

7. T. B. Macaulay, *The History of England from the Accession of James II*, ed. T. F. Henderson (London: George Routledge & Sons, 1907), p. 33.

8. W. C. Abbott, *The Writings and Speeches of Oliver Cromwell* (Cambridge, Mass.: Harvard University Press, 1939), II, 644. The occasion was the dissolution of the Long Parliament. For the same phrase compare Carlyle, *Letters and Speeches of Oliver Cromwell*, ed. Lomas, I, 398.

9. Carlyle, *Letters and Speeches of Oliver Cromwell*, ed. Lomas, I, 393–400.

10. *Ibid.*, III, 87.

11. This was the verdict of F. Guizot (*History of the English Revolution of 1640: From the Accession of Charles I to His Death* [London: Bell & Daldy, 1867], p. 38).

12. *The Works of John Owen*, ed. W. H. Goold (Edinburgh: T. & T. Clark, 1862), VIII, 279.

13. *Ibid.*, p. 381.

14. Edward, Earl of Clarendon, *History of the Rebellion*, ed. W. D. Macray (Oxford, 1888), VI, 70.

15. Carlyle, *Letters and Speeches of Oliver Cromwell*, ed. Lomas, II, 314 n.

16. See, e.g., the speeches to Parliament of September 12, 1654; January 22, 1655; and February 4, 1658 (*ibid.*, II, 367, 424–30; III, 187–92).

17. "The Enemy hath blocked up our way at the Pass at Copperspath, through which we cannot get without almost a miracle. He lieth so upon the Hills that we know not how to come that way without great difficulty; and our lying here daily consumeth our men, who fall sick beyond imagination. . . . Our spirits are comfortable (praised be the Lord) though our present condition be as

it is. And indeed we have much hope in the Lord; of whose mercy we have had large experience" (*ibid.*, II, 92).

18. The reference is to Exod. 2:14: "And he [the wrongdoer of the two] said [unto Moses], 'Who made thee a prince and a judge over us? Intendest thou to kill me, as thou killedst the Egyptian?' "

19. Cromwell to Fleetwood (*Letters and Speeches of Oliver Cromwell*, ed. Lomas, II, 307).

20. *Ibid.*, p. 123.

21. Abbott, *op. cit.*, IV, 871–72.

22. "The Ready and Easy Way To Establish a Free Commonwealth," *The Prose Works of John Milton*, ed. J. A. St. John (London: George Bell & Sons, 1909), I, 11.

23. Richard Baxter, *A Holy Commonwealth* (London, 1659), p. 175.

24. *An Excerpt from Reliquiae Baxterianae*, ed. Francis John, Bishop of Chester (London: Longmans, Green & Co., 1910), pp. 37–38.

CHAPTER VI

1. E.g., H. A. Taine, *L'Idéalisme anglais; étude sur Carlyle* (Paris: G. Baillière, 1864), p. 126: "There are many religions which are not at all moral, there are many more which are not at all practical. Carlyle wants to reduce the heart of man to the English sense of duty, and the imagination of man to the English sense of reverence. Half of human poetry escapes these bounds. For if one part of ourselves raises us to abnegation and virtue, another part leads us away to joy and pleasure. Man is pagan as well as Christian; Nature has two faces."

2. Lord Rosebery, *Miscellanies Literary and Historical* (2 vols.; London: Hodder & Stoughton, Ltd., 1921), I, 98–99.

3. *The Letters and Speeches of Oliver Cromwell, with Elucidations by Thomas Carlyle*, ed. S. C. Lomas (London: Methuen & Co., 1904), I, 462.

4. Mrs. Hale, *The Letters of Lady Mary Wortley Montagu* (Boston: Roberts Bros., 1869), p. 169.

5. *The Journal of the Rev. John Wesley* (4 vols.; "Everyman's Library" [London: J. M. Dent & Co., 1907]), I, 103.

6. Quoted in E. D. Bebb, *Nonconformity and Social and Economic Life 1600–1800* (London: Epworth Press, 1935), p. 64.

7. Quoted in J. C. Brauer, *Protestantism in America* (Philadelphia: Westminster Press, 1953), p. 204. The remark was Dwight L. Moody's.

8. H. C. Foxcroft, *Life and Works of the First Marquis of Halifax* (2 vols.; London: Longmans, Green & Co., 1898), II, 308.

9. Lyman Abbott, Amory H. Bradford, *et al.*, *The New Puritanism* (New York: Fords, Howard & Hulbert, 1898), p. 88.

Index

Gentry, rise of, 63–64
Goodwin, Thomas, 2–5
Gorton, Samuel, 46, 51–52, 57, 58–60

Halfway covenant, 35–36
Harrington, James, 63
Harrison, Thomas, 77, 78
Harvard College, 28–29
History, Puritan view of, 19–20
Hobbes, Thomas, 16
Holy community, objects of, 18
Hooker, Richard, 10
Hooker, Thomas, 29, 31
Humor, 110–11
Hutchinson, Anne, 28, 35, 46

Independents, 70–72, 84
Intellectual quality in Puritanism, 21, 106–7, 113
Ireton, Henry, 71, 75

Levellers, 58, 73–77
Long Parliament, 66, 82

Massachusetts, 19–38
Millenarianism, 42, 45, 54, 57, 75–79
Miller, Perry, 21, 30
Milton, John, 37, 43, 44, 45, 70, 75, 77, 96, 97
Montagu, Lady Mary Wortley, 104
Morison, Samuel Eliot, 28–29

New Haven, 19–38

Owen, John, 71, 77, 90–91

Parliamentary conflict in English Civil Wars, 62–67
Perkins, William, 3; catalogue of popular errors, 6–7
Plymouth, 19–38
Powell, Vavasor, 91–92
Presbyterians, the Puritan Right, 15, 67–70, 71, 82, 83, 84, 97, 98
Prophecy in New England, 27–28, 42, 49, 51–52, 58–60; *see also* Millenarianism
Protectorate, 86–97

Puritan party in England, composition of, 11–12, 41, 69–70

Quakers, 1, 43, 44, 45, 60

Radicalism in English Puritanism, 72–77; *see also* Levellers; Millenarianism
Regicide, 84–85
Religious experience; *see* Conversion experience
Religious liberty; *see* Freedom of worship
Republicanism, 56–58, 65, 72–77, 111–13
Revivals, 103–6
Rhode Island, 46–60
Rosebery, Earl of, 100–101

Salvation, doctrine of, 6–7; *see also* Conversion experience
Separation of church and state, 14–15, 41–46; in England, 70–71; in Massachusetts, 26; in Rhode Island, 46–60
Sewall, Samuel, 36
Sin, Puritan preoccupation with, 7–8, 91, 103
Social classes attracted to Puritanism, 11–12
"Soul liberty," 50, 53, 54, 55, 57, 74

Theocracy; *see* Civil government; Presbyterians, the Puritan Right
Toleration; *see* Freedom of worship
Tribalization of Puritan spirit in New England, 24–27, 34
Typology, 47, 49

Vane, Sir Henry, 43, 44, 45, 60, 66, 70, 77

Walker, Clement, 54–55
Wesley, Charles, 105
Wesley, John, 104–5
Williams, Roger, 46–51, 52, 57–58, 59, 70, 74, 108
Winthrop, John, 23–24